Winning the Worry War

WINNING
THE
WORRY
WAR

Formerly titled *Thank You Therapy*

Don Baker

VICTOR BOOKS

A DIVISION OF SCRIPTURE PRESS PUBLICATIONS INC.
USA CANADA ENGLAND

Unless otherwise indicated, Scripture quotations are from the *New American Standard Bible,* © the Lockman Foundation 1960, 1962, 1963, 1968, 1971, 1972, 1973, 1975, 1977. Used by permission. Other quotations are from the *Authorized (King James) Version* (KJV).

Copyediting: Greg Clouse
Cover Design: Larry Taylor

Recommended Dewey Decimal Classification: 248.4
Suggested Subject Heading: CHRISTIAN LIVING

Library of Congress Catalog Card Number: 89-60149
ISBN: 1-56476-057-x

2   3   4   5   6   7   8   9   10   11   Printing/Year   97   96   95   94   93

Contents

To all the world's anxious—
with the hope that this remedy for
your anxiety will be as helpful
to you as it has been to me.

"Anxiety in the heart of a man weighs it down."

Proverbs 12:25

CHAPTER ONE
That's Anxiety

I worry a lot.

Since worrying is something that spiritual people are not supposed to do, I don't call it that. I use words like

concerned,

troubled,

distressed,

fearful,

exercised, or even *disturbed.*

I also carefully avoid the word *anxious*. The Scriptures clearly prohibit anxiety since it seems to be just the opposite response from faith. And yet, even though I preach and teach about how to overcome fear, I've been described by people who should know as a person who is

anxiety-depressive,

obsessive-compulsive, and

as having a temperament that swings from choleric to melancholic.

I'm the sort of person who is late if he's not early,

who never does anything slowly, and

whose greatest irritation in life is having to wait

—for anything.

I'm a workaholic who'll probably never slow down,
a light sleeper whose brain begins racing the moment his
  eyes pop open,
an activist who'd rather attack a problem than understand it,
a type-A person who may have advanced slightly to a B+,
a bottom-liner who resists details,
a "now" person whose interests are not in the past *or* in the
  future, and
a perfectionist—in some areas of life anyway.

My publishers commend me on my manuscripts, my congregation compliments me on my sermons, and my staff congratulates me on my thoroughness—but please don't ask to look in my closets.

I'm sensitive—"supersensitive," some say. I'm so sensitive that I'm sensitive about my sensitivity. Friends insist that it's my greatest asset. They also claim that it's my greatest liability.

I'm in my 60s—and I'm not holding.

My cholesterol is too high.

My blood sugar is too low.

My heart beats too fast, and

my weight is 175 and dropping—and rising, and
dropping, and . . .

I'm cancer-prone, having already chalked up 2 surgeries and 33 biopsies. I'm also credited with one mild stroke.

I am not wealthy—or anywhere near it. I have no retirement program, no family inheritance, and I'm in debt.

I have never owned my own home and never will.

I carry credit cards that I shouldn't own and pay interest I can't afford.

When I'm writing a book like this one, I vanish. Both my mind and my body move into some netherworld, and I'm gone—until it's finished.

I'm anxiety-prone. I've taken tranquilizers to calm down and prescribed amphetamines to energize me.

I'm a terribly anxious person—or more accurately, I've been a terribly anxious person. I've made some progress—some significant progress, but I still occasionally suffer slight relapses.

•

Now, if you've lost confidence in my ability to help anyone suffering from anxiety, let me assure you—I'm an expert on the subject.

I know how it feels,
I know how it thinks,
I know its cause, and
I know its cure.
I know the cold, drenching sweat of anxiety.
I know the limp knees of anxiety.
I know the dry mouth,
the sweaty palms,
the shaky limbs,
the deep sighs,
the panic, and
the awesome feelings of impending doom.

I've experienced the ulcer, the spastic colon, and the anxiety pain in the pit of my stomach that felt like someone had touched me with a hot iron.

I've been anxious about life and I've been anxious about death.

I've allowed my anxiety over
unpaid bills,
unfinished work,
unprepared sermons,
unresolved conflicts, and
even unanswered phone calls
to grow to such proportions that I've wanted to just "chuck it all" and "check out."

I have even felt anxiety over my anxiety.

But I'm not alone. Everyone experiences anxiety. Anxiety has often been referred to as one of the most common 20th-century psychological problems. It is called the "official emotion of our age."

Rollo May, famed psychologist, has referred to anxiety as

"one of the most urgent problems of our day" (*The Meaning of Anxiety*, rev. ed., Norton, 1977, p. 9).

Everyone experiences anxiety, yet not everyone experiences it to the same degree.

MODERATE ANXIETY is normal and healthy when it causes us to avoid danger or when it heightens our efficiency. The awareness of a possible collision that causes me to slow down and stop at a busy intersection is normal and healthy. It subsides as soon as the stressful moment has passed.

CHRONIC ANXIETY that persists long after I've passed through the dangerous intersection is abnormal and unhealthy. Such anxiety may project its fear to every driving situation. It may even eventually cause me to fear driving or riding in an automobile.

I always experience normal or moderate anxiety over preaching. That NORMAL ANXIETY began as an obsessive fear when I was young and terribly afraid to stand before people and speak. The paralyzing fear eventually subsided through frequent preaching to the point that now public speaking only scares me a little. Years ago, during a major depressive illness, my NORMAL ANXIETY heightened to CHRONIC ANXIETY when I resisted preaching and withdrew from my pulpit responsibilities. On one particular Sunday it escalated to NEUROTIC ANXIETY that made routine preaching an impossibility.

Many who come for counseling come because of anxiety.

Bob was the 28-year-old driver of an 18-wheeler. His heart was healthy and whole, but he was so frightened of a possible fatal heart attack that he was immobilized.

That's anxiety.

Jill was the young mother of two small children. She was so concerned over getting enough rest to properly care for them that she couldn't sleep at night.

That's anxiety.

William was a successful general practitioner who gave up

his lucrative practice because he feared making a mistake.
That's anxiety.

Margaret was an effective Bible teacher who was so afraid
of failure that she became physically ill the day before each
teaching assignment.
That's anxiety.

Mark was a highly skilled mechanic whose fear of losing his
job was so great that he found himself incapable of performing
his duties.
That's anxiety.

Moses was a man of unparalleled talents and training who,
because of a speech impediment, resisted the call of God to
lead the Hebrews out of their Egyptian slavery (Exodus 4:10).
That's anxiety.

Jeremiah was a talented prophet whom God ordered to
preach to His rebellious people. Jeremiah initially resisted that
call with the complaint that he was too young for the job
(Jeremiah 1:6).
That's anxiety.

Isaiah withdrew from his responsibility to minister to that
same nation because he felt unworthy (Isaiah 6:5).
That's anxiety.

The Apostle Paul "had no rest in his spirit" because he
thought he had lost his traveling companion, Titus (2 Corinthians 2:12-13).
That's anxiety.

King David described his soul as "disturbed" or "disquieted"
(KJV) when he was forced to flee from his throne (Psalm 42:5,
11).
That's anxiety.

This same King David felt his vitality drained from him and his body wasting away because of sin-induced torment (Psalm 32:3-4).

That's anxiety.

Jesus was deeply troubled as He approached the time and place of His death (Mark 14:33-35).

That's anxiety.

Everyone experiences anxiety, but if that anxiety is not relieved or controlled, it can cause disorders of the digestive system,

> the circulatory system,
>> the nervous system,
>>> the glands,
>>>> the muscles and joints,
>>>>> the eyes, and
>>>>>> the skin.

I temporarily lost the use of both arms a few years ago. Extensive diagnostic studies revealed no neurologic or organic problems. I recovered the use of my arms with the resolution of a particularly stressful circumstance.

That's anxiety.

●

Anxiety is both psychological and physical. It begins in the emotions in the form of a fear. The fear may be real or imagined. It may be slight or it may be great—but it persists until the body begins to react to the perceived presence of undiminished fright. That reaction may be nothing more than the moistening of the palms or a sweaty brow. It may display itself in uncontrolled diarrhea.

That's anxiety.

Anxiety, though it can be recognized in both physical and psychological symptoms, is primarily a problem that is spiritual.

Anxiety left unchecked and uncontrolled is raw unbelief.

It is fear that refuses to respond to faith.

It is doubt that eventually displays itself as distress.

It is unbelief that ultimately renders a body unhealthy.

It is the unwillingness or inability to allow the abiding presence of an all-powerful God to take charge of any distressing circumstance in life.

I don't minimize the significant suggestions made by members of the medical profession. I don't discount the helpful therapeutic advice given by many competent counselors. I don't reject the importance of the many helpful controlled substances that are routinely prescribed. And I certainly don't ignore the beneficial self-help suggestions that I use and share with others. *But anxiety is essentially a spiritual problem.* It is referred to at least 32 times in Scripture. It is clearly discouraged by our Lord as being contrary to faith and is prohibited by the Apostle Paul when he says, "Be anxious for nothing" (Philippians 4:6).

Though God clearly teaches us to not be anxious, He is fully aware of humanity's predisposition to anxiety. Anxiety is not only the "official emotion of our day," it is the sin of the age. But God has freely offered us a solution.

It is prayer—but not just any kind of prayer. To say to an anxious person, "Pray about it," is often counterproductive. Some forms of prayer can even increase our anxiety. But to teach a person *how to pray about it* can ultimately result in significant relief.

It's a particular way of praying that is a literal response to a specific truth taught in one special passage in Scripture.

It's the biblical prescription for anxiety that's packaged right alongside the warning against anxiety in Philippians 4:6-7. It's God's antidote for most of the cares and concerns that are part of every person's complex, demanding lifestyle.

And it works.

●

It's good medicine that can be taken before, after, or even during meals.

It has absolutely no distressing side effects.

It can be taken with or without water.

It requires no prescription—not even a druggist.
It's foolproof and fail-safe—and it's free.
I call it THANK-YOU THERAPY.

●

It's designed to relieve the symptoms of anxiety, regardless
of how distressing they might be. It's even designed to erase
the cause of those symptoms.

Thank-You Therapy is the explanation of my survival of 38
years of demanding pastoral ministry. It explains the vigor that
allows me to still travel 100,000 miles a year, ministering to
pastors, churches, and missionaries all over the world.

It explains why this anxiety-prone, stress-filled person
hasn't quit.

It provides a living demonstration of how a weak person
replaces his weakness with divine strength by a simple act of
faith.

Let me explain it to you.

QUESTIONS TO REFLECT ON
1. To what extent are you now or have you ever been troubled with anxiety?
2. How does it affect you?
3. What concerns in your life give you the most anxiety?
4. How do you handle them?
5. Is your approach effective?
6. Do you agree that anxiety and unbelief are related?
7. How?

"Be anxious for nothing, but in everything by prayer and supplication with thanksgiving let your requests be made known to God. And the peace of God, which surpasses all comprehension, shall guard your hearts and your minds in Christ Jesus."

Philippians 4:6-7

CHAPTER TWO

The Transforming Power of Thankfulness

Read the entire passage carefully.

> Be anxious for nothing, but in everything by prayer and supplication *with thanksgiving* let your requests be made known unto God. *And* the peace of God, which surpasses all comprehension, shall guard your hearts and minds in Christ Jesus (Philippians 4:6-7).

The passage is almost too well known. All of us are familiar with its presence. Many of us have committed it to memory, but only a few of us have really grasped its meaning.

Let me be very basic and elementary—maybe even redundant—by reviewing some of the facts of the passage that we may already know.

WHO GAVE US THIS LITTLE GEM?

It's part of a very personal letter, written by the Apostle Paul to a small community of believers in the Macedonian city of Philippi, a town about 200 miles north of Athens.

WHY DID HE WRITE IT?

The Philippians were a congregation of anxious people.

They were ambitiously engaged in personal rivalries—each

attempting to achieve a position of superiority over the other.

They were caught in the very human tug-of-war between those who claim sinless perfection and those who encourage a do-as-you-please lifestyle.

They were being drowned in a sea of rules and regulations. A group of self-styled legalists wanted to wrench from them the high-priced freedom that Christ had already secured for them.

They were proud, arrogant, self-seeking, and indifferent to the needs of others. Nearly one fourth of this letter addresses the subject of humility—a humility that was almost impossible to find among the Philippian Christians.

And certainly not least among the Philippians' worries, they were under attack from nonbelievers.

So, what we had in ancient Philippi was the same set of anxiety-inducing problems that are found in most present-day congregations:

> rivalry, with its unbridled ambition;
> perfectionism, with its attendant frustration;
> loose living, with its crushing guilt;
> legalism, with its ugly hypocrisy; and
> persecution, with its ever-present fear.

Any of the above is sufficient reason for anxiety. Put them all together, and you have ANXIETY in capital letters.

To these anxiety-ridden people, Paul commands,

Be anxious for nothing.

That sounds like the ivory-towered, Pollyanna ravings of a demented being who is not only detached from reality, but who has taken either temporary or permanent leave of his senses.

"It is *impossible* to be free of anxiety under those circumstances," we say.

WHERE WAS PAUL WHEN HE WROTE THIS?

In Rome—in prison. He probably hadn't been taken yet to the Mammertine dungeon where he was ultimately beheaded;

but he was at least under house-arrest, probably confined, possibly even chained day and night to a Roman guard.

His evangelistic campaigns had been canceled.

His church-planting forays had ceased.

His visits to young believers had been stopped.

His freedom had been curtailed.

His future was uncertain.

His death seemed imminent.

His ministry was limited to dictating a few words each day to people he would probably never see—sending them to churches from which he possibly would never receive a response.

He could never know the impact of what he must have suspected was a very limited ministry.

HOW DID HE FEEL?

He wanted to die—but not enough to commit suicide, or even enough to allow an obsessive death wish to impair his senses. Nevertheless, he wanted to "depart and be with Christ," which he was convinced would be much better (Philippians 1:23).

So who we had in ancient Rome, authoring the four impossible words, "Be anxious for nothing," was an apostle

whose ministry had been cut short,

whose freedom had been taken from him,

whose body was chained to another,

whose heart was full of things to say that could be said only on paper,

whose productive life was finished, and

who was certain that his physical life was about to end.

That's the sort of person and that was the set of circumstances that gave birth to the words, "Be anxious for nothing."

As impossible as it seems, he still said it, and he meant it. He had learned the secret of an anxiety-free life. He employed the remedy constantly, and he shared it completely.

WHAT DOES PAUL PRESCRIBE FOR ANXIETY?

He gives us three ingredients, mixed together, each one

essential to the prescription's effectiveness.

The three parts are:

1. Be anxious for nothing.
2. Be prayerful for everything.
3. Be thankful for anything.

None by itself can lessen anxiety.

The command to be anxious for nothing is impossible to keep.

The exhortation to pray for everything is too common. Prayer can sometimes even increase anxiety.

The transforming ingredient is THANKSGIVING. Thanksgiving is the catalyst to this medication. Let me illustrate.

Remember, an anxiety attack is the result of negative thoughts that induce fear.

Let's say that you're a Philippian Christian who's been nominated to your church's board of elders—and there's nothing you want more than that position. The election is to be held tomorrow. You're just about to drop off to sleep when you remember that you have forgotten to solicit the vote of that one undecided member that would assure your victory—and it's too late to do anything about it.

I realize that this sounds like a very carnal illustration, but then this was a very carnal church, and that's the way ambitious people think when they're engaged in self-seeking rivalry. The very real possibility of losing a highly prized position is sufficient cause for extreme anxiety.

As you think of the possible loss of an election and your inability to do anything about it, the adrenalin begins flowing. Adrenalin always flows heavily in the presence of fear.

You break out in a cold sweat,
your eyes pop open wide,
your body twitches,
your mouth goes dry, and
you begin to toss in bed.

If you can recognize these as symptoms of anxiety, then you can employ Thank-You Therapy with almost immediate results.

If you cannot recognize anxiety, and you begin fearing an organic problem, then you will probably get even more frightened, produce more adrenalin, and experience even more disturbing bodily sensations.

It's important—it's basic to Thank-You Therapy—to be able to recognize anxiety when it strikes. If you do—and when you do—you are then ready to take the medicine Paul prescribed.

●

BE ANXIOUS FOR NOTHING.

The first step is to recognize anxiety and acknowledge it for what it is.

Anxiety is unbelief.

Anxiety is unacceptable to God.

Anxiety is the raw nerve of fear exposed.

Anxiety is lack of confidence in God.

Anxiety is the absence of faith—and
   "without faith it is impossible to please God" (Hebrews 11:6).

Anxiety is sin.

Jesus repeatedly admonished us not to be anxious about
   what we're going to eat or
   what we're going to drink or
   what we're going to wear (Matthew 6:25).

He tells us that anxiety can change nothing (Matthew 6:27).

He reminds us of God's gracious provision for all His creation (Matthew 6:28-30).

He states that anxiety is characteristic of unbelievers (Matthew 6:32).

He says we don't even need to be anxious about tomorrow (Matthew 6:34).

And that's what you're anxious about—the outcome of tomorrow's election.

Peter tells us to deliberately let go of our anxieties, to cast "all your anxiety upon Him for He cares for you" (1 Peter 5:7).

After recognizing that your problem is anxiety and that anxiety is unbelief, then the next step is to pray.

BE PRAYERFUL FOR EVERYTHING.

"But in *everything* by prayer and supplication . . . let your requests be made known to God."

When Peter tells us to cast all our anxiety on Him (Christ), he is telling us to pray. Prayer is letting go. It's many other things too, but it's letting go—giving up—handing off—casting away our cares in God's direction.

Two words in Philippians 4:6 deal with prayer. The word *prayer* itself is a general word that covers the idea of prayer in its widest meaning. The word *supplication* is more specific. It refers to a special petition for some particular need.

As you lie in the darkness, vainly trying to sleep, you realize that anxiety over the outcome of tomorrow's election is keeping you awake.

You admit to yourself that your anxiety is wrong, and you begin to pray. Your prayer is probably nothing out of the ordinary. It may begin:

Dear Heavenly Father . . .

It may continue with words of worship and praise, but I doubt it. We're seldom worshipful when we're anxious. We're even less worshipful when we're sleepy. You may pray something like:

"I've got a problem" or

"I can't sleep. Lord, please help me to go to sleep" or

"Lord, I'm anxious. Please take away my anxiety."

The problem with this sort of praying is that you'll probably find that you have only increased your problem. You're wider awake than ever, and you're more anxious than when you began.

You've "let go" of nothing. Actually, you have only succeeded in heightening your anxiety by dwelling on it. Besides, you've added still another anxious fear with the realization that God hasn't honored your request.

"Letting go" is the act of honestly analyzing your fear and then verbally transferring that concern to God.

Your prayer could sound something like this:

> Dear Heavenly Father, I can't sleep. I'm feeling anxiety about tomorrow's election. I really want to win—but since there is nothing I can do about it tonight, I'm going to give this worry to You. It's no longer mine; it's Yours.
>
> In Jesus' name.

That is prayer and that is supplication. It is also letting go.

It may not be the way you'd say it—it may not even be the way I'd say it—but that's prayer.

But it's still not Thank-You Therapy. Thank-You Therapy includes a prayer of thanksgiving.

•

BE THANKFUL FOR ANYTHING.

Thank-You Therapy reads Philippians 4:6 carefully—

> Be anxious for nothing, but in everything by prayer and supplication *with thanksgiving* let your requests be made known unto God.

Remember, it's
> anxious for nothing,
> > prayerful for everything,
> > > thankful for anything.

To complete the process, your prayer might sound something like this:

> Dear Heavenly Father, I can't sleep. I'm anxious about the election tomorrow and I know I shouldn't be. I really want to win, but since there is nothing I can do about it tonight, I'm going to give this worry to You. It's no longer mine; it's Yours.

But it doesn't stop there. It continues:

Thank You for hearing me as You've promised.
Thank You for understanding my dreams and my desires.
Thank You for loving me in spite of my carnal ambitions.
Thank You for already knowing the outcome of tomorrow's election and for having the power to cause it to go either way.
Thank You, Father, that whatever happens, it will be Your will, and it will be for my good.

In Jesus' name,
Amen.

That's Thank-You Therapy.

Your thank-you may be shorter or longer or simpler or more profound. Still it is designed to accomplish the same thing—to thank God, in advance, for taking your concern as He promised and then doing with it whatever is in your best interest.

The next step is God's.

In response to your prayer, supplication, and thanksgiving, He promises that

The *peace* of God, which surpasses all comprehension, shall *guard* your hearts and your minds in Christ Jesus.

Anxiety and peace are opposites.
They are incompatible.
They cannot coexist in the same mind.
They cannot dwell together in the same heart.
The turmoil of anxiety must give way to the serenity of peace.
And that peace, according to Philippians 4:7, is
    indefinable,
        indescribable, and
            incomprehensible.

It's the divine tranquilizer that brings supernatural relaxation to a troubled brain.

It's better than Nytol, Sominex, or even Valium.

When our imaginary Philippian, or any anxious believer, employs it, it works.

When I employ it, especially at night when my mind gets overcrowded with anxious thoughts, I'm surprised and delighted every time to find that the next thing I know, it's morning.

QUESTIONS TO REFLECT ON
1. Have you committed Philippians 4:6-7 to memory?
2. If you think I'm placing too much importance on the word *thanksgiving*, what alternative explanation do you have for its presence in this passage?
3. Do you agree that anxiety is a sin?
4. What anxious thought can you locate for which you can test this suggestion?
5. What were the results?

"When my anxious thoughts multiply within me, Thy consolations delight my soul."
Psalm 94:19

CHAPTER THREE
The Giant Step of Faith

Thank-You Therapy is an act of faith.

The ultimate objective of our Heavenly Father is to bring us to a place of unwavering confidence in Him.

To thank God for the answer before it's received—

To thank God for what He will do as well as for what He has done—

To thank God on the basis of a promise rather than the fulfillment of a request—

is an act of faith, a giant step in the direction of complete and unwavering confidence.

Thank-You Therapy is prayer coupled together with thanksgiving (Philippians 4:6-7).

●

One of the most anxiety-ridden moments in all of human history took place in a little Galilean town called Nazareth, nestled in the hills overlooking Israel.

A first-century teenager named Mary was suddenly and unexpectedly informed that she was about to become pregnant—before marriage! An angel told her that despite her pregnancy, she would remain a virgin. What's more, Mary learned that it would not be kept a secret—in fact, eventually the whole world would know about it.

Premarital pregnancies were not only immoral in ancient Israel; they were illegal. They were not only grounds for the dissolution of a marriage contract; they were often just cause for abandonment and death.

To an orthodox Hebrew, pregnancy outside marriage was unthinkable.

These were the days before Planned Parenthood clinics and crazy abortion-on-demand laws. In fact, in Mary's day, a young girl who became pregnant was even expected to tell her parents.

The truth of Mary's miraculous conception would be just as unbelievable in 1st-century Israel as it would be today in 20th-century America.

Mary was anxious.

Luke, in his Gospel account, tells us that when God's special angel made this extraordinary announcement to Mary,

    she was greatly troubled (Luke 1:29),

    she couldn't get it out of her mind (verse 29),

    she was afraid (verse 30),

    she couldn't believe it (verse 34) and,

    she even ran away from home (verses 39-40).

Runaways were also unheard of in the land of the sons of Abraham, but then what else could a young girl do who feared the wrath of a skeptical father and the ravings of an hysterical mother? She certainly couldn't tell Joseph, her husband-to-be.

She went about as far as a person could go—75 miles to the outer limits of Israel's only big city, and she told

        the only one who would listen,

           the only one who didn't fear,

                the only one who might possibly understand—

            she told her cousin, Elizabeth.

Such news traveled fast in Mary's day—just as it does in our day. Elizabeth already knew. Elizabeth's unborn baby already knew, and in a remarkable experience of prenatal communication, Mary relaxed and believed that God was about to do something very special (Luke 1:41-45).

She still had only a promise. But on the basis of that promise she pulled 15 appropriate Old Testament quotations from her memory, framed them into a marvelous song of praise, and with it offered her thanksgiving to God (Luke 1:46-55)—
before Joseph knew,
before her family knew,
nine months before Jesus was born, and
years before the truth would ever become known.
That's Thank-You Therapy.

Thank-You Therapy thanks God for the answer before it's received,

Thank-You Therapy thanks God for what He will do rather than for what He has done, and

Thank-You Therapy thanks God on the basis of a promise rather than the fulfillment of a request.

Thank-You Therapy asks God to meet a need and then thanks Him before the need has been met—thanks Him on the basis of a promise already given.

●

Abraham did a similar thing.

Childless and homeless, he listened to a promise that was about as farfetched and unthinkable as any promise could be— a promise that assured him that he would eventually own all the land his eyes could see and gather a family whose descendants would number more than could be counted.

Just a promise, but Abraham built an altar and offered thanks before the promise's fulfillment.

Thank-You Therapy accepts a promise with as much certainty as its fulfillment—*if* the promise is made by God.

That's faith, and Thank-You Therapy is an act of faith.

●

The parents of a teenager were greatly troubled over the unexplainable change that had come over their daughter.

She had become distant,
sullen,
rebellious,
unloving, and

indifferent to the things of God.

This was the same girl they had dedicated to Christ at birth, the same girl who'd invited Jesus into her heart as a child, and who had always displayed a gentle, caring, loving spirit, intent on someday entering Christian ministry.

The anxiety level ran high.

"What did we do wrong?"

"What didn't we do right?"

"What has happened?"

"What will happen?"

"What can we do?"

"What should we do?"

The questions were endless.

The pain was unrelieved.

The problem went unsolved.

I tried every conceivable way to encourage them, to reassure them, and to relieve the overwhelming feelings of guilt.

Finally I pointed them to a promise—a promise just as real as the one made to Mary and just as valid as the one given to Abraham.

It's a promise that has its origin in God and that has all the weight of heaven behind it—a promise that has sustained me for all my years in ministry. It's Philippians 1:6—

> For I am confident of this very thing, that He who began a good work in you will perfect it until the day of Christ Jesus.

That's not an isolated statement in Scripture. A similar promise is made in Psalm 138:8—

> The Lord will accomplish what concerns me.

The same idea is expressed in Romans 8:29-30—

> For whom He foreknew, He also predestined to become conformed to the image of His Son, that He

might become the firstborn among many brethren; and whom He predestined, these He also called; and whom He called, these He also justified; and whom He justified, these He also glorified.

Don't get hung up on the theological jargon of Romans 8. Like hundreds of other promises in Scripture, it simply states that God has an unchangeable plan for all those who are His.

We agreed, as these dear parents and I talked about their girl, that God had started a work in her life. The evidences of the Spirit's presence were too numerous to be ignored.

I encouraged them, on the basis of Philippians 1:6, to stop praying the prayer of anxiety and to start using Thank-You Therapy.

Their prayer changed from

"Father, do something to bring our daughter back to Yourself" to

"Father, thank You that You are at work in our daughter's life and that You are going to do what needs to be done—in Your way and in Your time."

That's Thank-You Therapy.

It's the prayer of thanksgiving that's offered before circumstances change, even in spite of the fact that circumstances may worsen.

It's a prayer of thanksgiving that's prayed on the basis of a promise rather than the fulfillment of a request.

•

The Christian ministry produces its share of anxiety.

One of my most anxious moments came each time I stepped behind the pulpit to preach.

My prayers used to start out—

"Father, be with me."

"Father, help me."

"Father, strengthen me."

"Father, don't let me fail."

"Father, bless my ministry, etc., etc., etc."

Those prayers, rather than relieving my anxiety, actually fed it. They constantly reminded me of the possibility of a humiliating failure. They caused me stress. They lacked confidence—they only reminded me of my weakness.

I would leave my study praying for help; I would walk to the platform distracted by fear, and I would go through the early part of the service in anguish.

Then I began believing some Bible promises like—

Do not fear, for I am with you;
do not anxiously look about you,
    for I am your God.
I will strengthen you,
surely I will help you,
surely I will uphold you with My
    righteous right hand (Isaiah 41:10)—

or God's promise to never desert us nor forsake us (Hebrews 13:5), or Jesus' promise to be with us always, even to the end of the age (Matthew 28:20).

I began to better understand the ministry of the "Helper," the Holy Spirit, and to grasp God's changeless desire to bless me. As a result, my prayer preparation for those crisis moments changed.

Rather than asking God to do something He'd already promised, I began thanking Him for what He was going to do.

"Thank You, Father, for the message You've given me."

"Thank You, Father, for being with me."

"Thank You, for the power of Your Holy Word."

"Thank You for the presence of Your Holy Spirit."

"Thank You for what You're going to do in this service."

I was released from anxiously praying for things already promised and was enabled to pray for those about to listen.

I began to worship rather than agonize.

I started noticing people and was able to begin ministering to them even before I started preaching.

That was Thank-You Therapy.

I began thanking God on the basis of a promise rather than the fulfillment of a request.

That's faith.

You see, according to Hebrews 11:1, faith is the conviction of realities I cannot see or feel.

A promise from God is a reality. It need not be visible or tangible. It need only be from God to be real.

Thank-You Therapy anchors itself in one of God's appropriate promises and then praises Him, in advance, for its fulfillment.

●

Thank-You Therapy thanks God for the answer before it is received.

Thank-You Therapy thanks God for what He will do as well as for what He has done.

Thank-You Therapy thanks God on the basis of a promise rather than the fulfillment of a request.

QUESTIONS TO REFLECT ON
1. Have you ever considered the ratio of thanksgiving to supplication in your praying?
2. Is it fairly proportionate?
3. Are you familiar enough with God's promises to effectively use them in your praying?
4. What urgent concern is troubling you today?
5. Is there a Bible promise already given you that pertains to that concern?
6. Can you lay that promise alongside that anxiety and thank God in advance for what He has already said He would do?

"There is anxiety by the sea, it cannot be calmed."

Jeremiah 49:23

CHAPTER FOUR
Accepting the Circumstances

Thank-You Therapy is an act of faith in the sovereignty of God.

Thank-You Therapy is not a psychological tool designed to lessen the impact of life's problems; it's a spiritual truth determined to refocus our attention.

It's not intended to change circumstances; its purpose is to change attitudes.

Thank-You Therapy is prayer coupled with thanksgiving (Philippians 4:6-7).

•

"But you don't know how it feels to look like this."

Those were the words of a 32-year-old woman confined to a body the size of a baby's—and yet different from a baby's. I first noticed her after speaking to a group of singles. She was seated on a couch with her tiny body propped up on a pillow. She had no legs and no arms. She had never had any legs or arms. There was a small deformed finger stretching out from her right shoulder. It was the only appendage on her body. Her head was normal. Her hair was light brown. Her face was attractive. Her smile was completely disarming.

I walked over to her and asked her name.

"Carol," she replied.

"I'm glad to meet you, Carol. Tell me," I asked, "how do you get from that place on the couch into your electrically operated wheelchair? Does somebody have to lift you?"

She smiled at my curiosity. "No, nobody has to lift me. I'll show you."

With that, she began energetically wiggling herself up onto the arm of the couch, stretched across the couch arm and then proceeded, wormlike, onto the seat of her wheelchair. Slowly she struggled, without help, into an upright position, pushed and pulled herself against the back of the chair, and triumphantly said, "There—nothing to it."

She was open and friendly. I was deeply curious.

I sat down beside her, studied her carefully, and asked, "What happened, Carol?"

"I was born like this."

"What caused it?"

"I don't really know."

"Were you a thalidomide baby?"

"It's possible," she said.

I had never seen a thalidomide baby, but I had read about them and had seen pictures of some of the hideous deformities caused when expectant mothers ingested a drug that was supposed to eliminate morning sickness. Thousands of unborn babies were affected in the 1950s in Europe and the United States. Most of them died.

"Are you in school?"

"Yes, I'm in my seventh year of college."

"How are your grades?"

"I'm passing—with difficulty, but I'm passing."

"How much can you do by yourself?"

"Quite a bit. Probably more than you think, but I do need help most of the time."

"How do you feel about yourself?"

"Sometimes I feel cheated," she said.

"Will you ever be able to get married?"

"I'd like to."

"Can you bear children?"

"No."

"What's the most difficult thing you do each day?"

"Look in the mirror. There are times when I feel almost normal. Then I take a look at myself. Sometimes it literally makes me sick."

"Have you ever asked God to work a miracle in your body and suddenly provide you with instant legs and arms?"

"Oh yes. That was my daily prayer when I was younger."

"Do you still ask for that?"

"No. For a long time I asked to die. You don't know what it feels like to live in a body like this."

"Don't you ask to die any longer?"

"No."

"Why?"

"I learned something—something about God that changed my life. Since that time, I'm still limited—I'm still crippled—I'm still deformed, but I'm at peace."

"What did you learn?"

A small group of fascinated bystanders drew closer to the little circle of friends and listened in silence.

"I learned that God made me this way," she said.

"God made you like that?" I asked.

"Well, not really. God never makes anything that looks like this. Everything God makes is perfect. No, God didn't make me like this, but God allowed me to be born this way. And if God allowed me to be born this way, it must have been for a purpose. When I realized that God allowed me to be born this way, I stopped complaining and began praising Him."

"How did you learn that? Did someone teach it to you?"

"No, I don't think so. I'm sure many people tried, but I just couldn't accept it. One day I had my Bible propped up in front of me. I was reading the Book of Job and feeling sorry for myself. As I turned the pages with a pencil clamped between my teeth, I suddenly realized that Job's hideous pain was no accident. Neither was it caused by God. But God allowed it. Nothing happens in the life of one of God's children without first receiving God's permission. God could have stopped all that was happening to Job—He can do that, you know," she said with a twinkle in her eye—"but He didn't. He could have given me a beautiful, healthy, normal body, but He didn't. When I realized that, I stopped fighting and pleading. I began just praising Him and thanking Him—and do you know what's happened?"

"No, what's happened?" I asked.

"I'm at peace."

She laughed as if she had discovered earth's best-kept secret. Her friends applauded.

I said, "Thank You, Father" for another example of a life-changing truth.

•

Thank-You Therapy is not a psychological tool designed to lessen the impact of life's problems; it's a spiritual truth determined to refocus our attention.

It's not intended to change circumstances; its purpose is to change attitudes. It's not life's circumstances that create anxiety; it's our own responses to them.

Most of us don't like what we see when we look in the mirror. We don't have to be deformed to be discontent.

Anáis Nin, noted psychologist and author, has said that everyone of us carries a deforming mirror where we see ourselves too small or too large, too fat or too thin. *USA Today* recently reported that nearly everyone is dissatisfied with some part of his body. Most people are unhappy with the size or the shape of their stomachs.

Me? I'm freckled—universally freckled. In fact, there's hardly a freckle anywhere on my body that isn't touching another freckle. As a boy, I would complain about them, pick at them, rub them, and persistently plead for some sort of salve or cream that would remove them.

I would wear long sleeves, high collars, and full-length trousers to cover them. I prayed every night that God would remove my freckles. I envied my brothers and sister because of the absence of blemishes on their skin. At times I was angry—but usually I was just embarrassed and sorry.

That's anxiety.

There might be some remedies for skinny legs and fat legs and skinny tummies and fat tummies. It's possible to cover bald spots and color graying hair. Even sagging facial muscles can be transformed through surgery. But freckles—they're for life. A deformed body—that's for life.

There are some things in life that can't be changed. They're as permanent and changeless as the loss of a limb or the loss of a loved one. They're for life.

Moses didn't have something as critical as a deformed body or something as simple as freckles. He had a speech problem that limited and embarrassed him every time he opened his mouth. He'd probably had it most of his life.

As he spoke to God through the burning bush at the base of Mount Sinai, he said, "I have never been eloquent... I am slow of speech and slow of tongue" (Exodus 4:10).

We don't know whether Moses stuttered or stammered or just had difficulty with pronunciation. All he tells us is that he spoke too slowly. He felt too limited by his difficulty to become Israel's leader. He lacked confidence in his speech, in his ability, in himself—like most of us.

In responding to Moses, God revealed a fact about Himself that provides us with the one truth that's basic to our understanding of Thank-You Therapy. He asked Moses:

> Who has made man's mouth? Or who makes him dumb
> or deaf, or seeing or blind? Is it not I, the Lord?
> (Exodus 4:11)

In those stunning words, God is accepting full responsibility for all that happens to man. He is saying that it is He who must bear the blame for a person's inability to hear, to speak, or to see. In those words, God assumes full and final responsibility for all that happens—in this world and in this life.

That is what is meant by the word *sovereign*. Sovereignty is the act of God's authority—His control—His supremacy in command of everything.

    Sovereignty is God's rule and overrule over all.

    Sovereignty is God's freedom to do
      as He pleases,
        when He pleases,
          with whom He pleases.

That's the remarkable lesson of the Book of Job. *Sovereign* means that God was free to do with Job exactly as He pleased.

That's a hard truth—not hard necessarily to understand but hard to accept.

The Apostle Paul addresses God's sovereignty in Romans 9. He states that the ultimate, final decision on any subject rests with God.

> Why did God choose Jews and not Gentiles to be His favored ones? (verses 3-5)

> Why did God choose the older brother Esau to serve the younger brother Jacob when this was contrary to both law and custom? (verses 10-13)

> Why does God have mercy on some and not on others? (verse 15)

> Why did He raise up Pharaoh for the ultimate purpose of destroying him? (verses 17-18)

> Doesn't the potter have any rights over the clay? Can't he mold it any way he chooses? (verses 20-21)

> If He wants to mold some clay into a valuable vase and other clay into a crockpot, isn't that His privilege? (verses 20-21)

Sovereignty allows God to be God.

Sovereignty permits God the freedom to act
    when He pleases,
      where He pleases,
        as He pleases, and
          with whom He pleases.

God is limited by a nature that refuses to act out of character with itself.

Sovereignty can raise up a Jacob and put down an Esau.

Sovereignty can raise up a Hebrew and put down a Gentile.

Sovereignty can raise up a Job and then put down that same Job.

Sovereignty can raise up a Pharaoh and then put that same Pharaoh down.

Sovereignty can cause life; it can withhold life.

Sovereignty can cause success; it can withhold success.

Sovereignty can cause good health; it can withhold good health.

Because—

Sovereignty allows God to be God. It gives Him the freedom to do

as He pleases,

when He pleases,

with whom He pleases.

Sovereignty gives God the freedom to allow

physical deformities or whole bodies,

freckled skin or skin free of blemishes.

Sovereignty means that God is free to be God.

Hard to understand?

No! It's not hard; it's impossible. I've always had difficulty understanding it—but I do accept it. It's the truth that enables me to say thank you to the One who allowed whatever it is that's the cause of my anxiety and to know that He could have controlled it if He wished. Since He didn't, then I can accept the fact that infinite wisdom and unchanging love conspired with Almighty power to cause something that's ultimately for my good and His glory.

I remember the first time I actually thanked God for my freckles.

Someone had pointed me to Leviticus 13:38-39:

And when a man or a woman has bright spots on the
skin of the body, even white bright spots, then the

> priest shall look, and if the bright spots on the skin of
> their bodies are a faint white, it is eczema [*a freckled
> spot* says the King James Version] that has broken out
> on the skin; he is clean.

That passage offered no explanation for freckles. It didn't en-
hance the beauty or increase the value of my freckles one bit.

It just said to me that God knows all about freckles, and He
made special provision for freckled people 3,500 years ago.

I laughed and said, "Thank You, Father, for my freckles. I
don't know why I have them, but I do know You've allowed
them."

That's Thank-You Therapy, and the therapy has worked.
I'm not only at peace with my freckles, I'm sort of proud of
them.

●

Thank-You Therapy will probably never be thankful for a
thalidomide body, but Thank-You Therapy can be thankful for
a sovereign God that doesn't allow for such problems without
good reason.

Thank-You Therapy is not a psychological tool designed to
lessen the impact of life's problems; it's a spiritual truth determined to refocus our attention.

It's not intended to change circumstances. Its purpose is to
change attitudes.

Thank-You Therapy gives thanks *in everything*—not necessarily *for everything*—for the sovereign wisdom that has allowed the circumstance and the unexplained reasons behind it.

Thank-You Therapy lifts the gaze of the human spirit to the
superhuman God, refocuses our attention from circumstances
to sovereignty, and then proclaims:

> Oh, the depth of the riches both of the wisdom and
> knowledge of God! How unsearchable are His judg-
> ments and unfathomable His ways! (Romans 11:33)

QUESTIONS TO REFLECT ON
1. What physical or emotional imperfections are you aware of in your life?
2. Are you anxious about them?
3. Can you do anything to change them?
4. Have you been able yet to say, "Thank You, Father"?
5. If not, why not?

Anxiety focuses on self and has its roots in unbelief. Peace focuses on God and has its roots in faith.

CHAPTER FIVE

Standing On the Promises

Thank-You Therapy is faith in the forgiving grace of God.

Thank-You Therapy acts on a promise, not on a feeling.

It accepts a truth regardless of how impossible or implausible it may seem.

It says "Thank You" for a reality without having to secure it with logic or evidence.

●

"I'm not really sure that I'm going to heaven when I die."

Those were the quiet words that came from an apprehensive male voice late one Sunday evening.

The phone call had interrupted some relaxed moments as I sought to unwind from a very busy Sunday. The caller was apologetic, but he needed to talk.

"I don't know quite how to start," he began. "I was in church tonight, and I came away quite troubled. You said that if you died tonight, you know that you'd go to heaven to be with Christ, and I can't say that—but I want to be able to."

I moved to another phone and asked, "Do I know you?"

"I don't think so. My name is Steve. I attend the church regularly but I haven't joined yet. I'm a student at the seminary."

"You must have had a difficult time making this call, Steve. It's not often that I get a phone call from a seminary student who is unsure of his salvation."

"I did have a hard time. I don't know how many times I've dialed your number and then chickened out. I've never told this to anyone, and I must admit that I'm ashamed to admit it to you—but I had to talk to someone."

"Well, if it's any comfort to you, Steve, you've called the right person. I had been licensed to preach the Gospel for two years before I really knew for certain that God had forgiven my sins. I can still remember the terrible anxiety that came from not being sure, and the embarrassment that wouldn't allow me to admit it to anyone. What makes you think you're not a Christian?"

"For years now, every time I hear a sermon that talks about sin, salvation, or eternal life, I want to respond all over again. My pastor used to really come on strong during an invitation to receive Christ. When he did, I was in agony. My hands would perspire; in fact, I'd break out in a cold sweat all over, and I just wanted to run. I don't know whether you can believe this or not, but I even share Christ with others. When I do, I must admit that when I'm telling them what Jesus Christ can do for them, I have a gnawing doubt way down somewhere deep inside me. I really wonder if what I'm saying is true. I'm not sure He's done that for me."

That's anxiety.

"Steve," I said, "do you mind if I ask you some very basic— even elementary—questions?"

"No, go ahead. I think that's what I need."

"In the first place, you can be encouraged with the fact that I seldom find a non-Christian who is concerned about his salvation. First Corinthians 2:14 reminds us that—

A natural man does not accept the things of the Spirit of God; for they are foolishness to him, and he cannot understand them, because they are spiritually appraised.

"Concern about spiritual things doesn't originate with Satan or even with the flesh," I reminded Steve. "The Holy Spirit is the One who takes spiritual thoughts and puts them together with spiritual words and produces spiritual concerns. First Corinthians 2:13 says so.

"Be encouraged, Steve. The fact that you're concerned may suggest the indwelling presence of the Spirit of God.

"Tell me, when did you receive Christ as your own personal Saviour?"

"When I was 10 years old."

"Where were you?"

"In Sunday School in my home church."

"Who pointed you to Christ?"

"My Sunday School teacher."

"What do you remember about that moment?"

"Well, my parents were Christians. I had gone with them to Sunday School and church all my life. That Sunday my teacher talked about John 3:16 and about how Jesus had died for our sins so that we didn't have to go to hell. She asked, 'How many of you want to go to heaven?'

"We all raised our hands.

"She told us that if we really wanted to go to heaven, to stay after class and she'd talk to us.

"I was the only one who stayed."

"What did you do then?" I asked.

"I prayed and asked Jesus to come into my life."

"Were you sincere?"

"I think so. I'm not really sure how sincere a 10-year-old is about anything, but I think I really meant it."

"What happened then?"

"I told my parents. A few Sundays later I joined a special class for new Christians and then was baptized."

"When did you begin doubting your Christian faith?"

"I think it was during my high school years. I wasn't wild or anything like that, but I wasn't perfect either. I just couldn't believe that anyone who thought and lived like I did could ever go to heaven."

"Did you talk to anyone about this?"

"No. My parents and my pastor all thought I was a Christian. In fact, they all thought I was about the most promising young Christian in the church. I was too embarrassed to mention it to anyone."

"What do you do when you get the feeling that you're not a Christian?"

"I agonize—a lot. I pray. I ask God over and over again to forgive me. I ask Him to give me some sort of sign that I'm a Christian. I tell Him that if I'm not a Christian to please make me one."

"What happens?"

"Nothing. I just feel worse. I figure that the fact that God doesn't answer is even greater proof that I'm not a believer. I've even thought of changing churches or even religions in the hope it might help."

I asked him if he knew of any presently unconfessed sin in his life. We both knew how sin can rob us of the positive feelings of a secure relationship.

"You do know, Steve, that God wants you to be sure of your relationship with Him. Your present confusion is not the will of God for your life. In 1 John 5:13 that fact is stated:

> These things have I written to you who believe in the
> name of the Son of God, in order that you may know
> that you have eternal life.

"And again in Romans 8:16 God's word tells us that He has given us His Holy Spirit in order that we may know that we are the children of God."

"I know that, Pastor. I do believe that God wants me to be sure of my salvation. Why then am I not?"

"Let's check the facts, Steve. Do you believe that by one man's disobedience sin passed to all men so that all are sinners, including yourself?" (Romans 5:12, 17, 19; 3:23)

"Yes."

"Do you believe that Jesus Christ, who was God in human

flesh, died to pay the penalty for all sin, including yours?" (Romans 5:8; 8:34; 1 Corinthians 15:3; Colossians 1:20-23; Hebrews 9:11-14; 10:10-14)

"Yes."

"Did you ask God for forgiveness of your sin? (Ephesians 1:7; Colossians 1:14; 1 John 1:9)

"Did He forgive you?"

"I think so."

"Did you invite Jesus Christ into your life?" (Revelation 3:20)

"Yes."

"Did He come into your life?"

"I think so, but that's where I'm not sure."

"If He didn't forgive you, and if He didn't move into your life, then what more is there for you to do in order to secure His forgiveness?"

"I don't think there's anything more for me to do."

"And if the blood of Jesus Christ isn't adequate to cleanse you from your sin, what else is there?"

"Nothing," he answered.

"Steve, you're right where I was in my thinking many years ago. I had done all that the Scriptures had told me to do; I had invited Christ into my life and had put my faith in His sacrificial death for my sins, but still lacked peace. So what did I do next?"

It was then that I referred Steve to Philippians 4:6-7.

> Be anxious for nothing, but in everything by prayer and supplication with thanksgiving let your requests be made known to God. And the peace of God, which surpasses all comprehension, shall guard your hearts and your minds in Christ Jesus.

I realized at that moment that what I wanted and needed was not salvation, but peace. I was anxious. Anxiety focuses on self and has its roots in unbelief. Peace focuses on God and has its roots in faith.

I developed the exercise of Thank-You Therapy. I began working my way through God's salvation promises. Instead of asking for something I already had, I began thanking Him for something He had already promised.

For instance, I took 1 John 1:9 and made it the object of Thank-You Therapy.

> If we confess our sins, He is faithful and righteous to forgive us our sins and to cleanse us from all unrighteousness.

I asked God again to forgive me, and then in spite of a continuing awareness of guilt, and in spite of not feeling forgiven, I thanked Him for forgiving me.

Thank-You Therapy acts on a promise, not on a feeling.

I took Revelation 3:20 and made it the object of Thank-You Therapy.

> Behold, I stand at the door and knock; if anyone hears My voice and opens the door, I will come in to him, and will dine with him, and he with Me.

I invited Jesus again to come into my life, and then on the basis of His promise, I thanked Him for moving into my life.

That's Thank-You Therapy—and that's God's remedy for the anxiety bred by unbelief.

●

There are an uncountable number of objective truths that find their fulfillment in each of us the moment we trust Christ—regardless of how we feel or think. A profitable exercise is to take each one of these, personalize them, pray about them, and thank God that each one is a reality—even if you have difficulty believing it.

When I trusted Jesus Christ as my personal Saviour,

I became forever joined to Christ (Romans 6:5).

I was freed from the penalty of the Law (Romans 7:4-6).

I became a child of God (John 1:12-13).

I was born again (1 Peter 1:23).
I was brought to life spiritually (Ephesians 2:5).
I was adopted into God's family (Ephesians 1:4-5).
I was made acceptable to God (Ephesians 1:6).
I was declared righteous (2 Corinthians 5:21).
I was set apart to God (1 Corinthians 6:11).
I was justified forever (Romans 5:1).
I was brought close to God (Ephesians 2:13).
I was delivered from darkness (Colossians 1:13).
I was brought into God's kingdom (1 Thessalonians 2:12).
I became a citizen of heaven (Philippians 3:20).
I was united to all believers (1 Corinthians 12:12-13).
I became a partner with Christ (1 John 5:11-12).
I became vitally linked to the Father (Romans 8:16).
I became vitally linked to the Son (Colossians 1:27).
I became vitally linked to the Spirit (Romans 5:5).
I was sealed by the Spirit (Ephesians 4:30).
I was empowered by the Spirit (Ephesians 5:18).
I was made complete in Christ (Colossians 2:9-10).
I was given every spiritual blessing (Ephesians 1:3).
I was promised life after death (1 Thessalonians 4:13-18).
I was promised life forever (John 3:16).
I was promised a resurrected body (1 Thessalonians 4:13-18).

These and other truths comprise part of the long list of things God did in us and for us the moment we trusted His Son Jesus.

I suggested to Steve that he begin working through this list. He should personalize each truth and then thank God for what had already been accomplished. I suggested he make it a daily routine, and daily thank God for what He had already done, rather than to continue to ask God for something He'd already promised.

•

A few weeks later I answered the phone and heard, "It

works—it works!" I didn't know who was calling or what he was talking about. Finally my caller identified himself. It was Steve, and he was telling me that for the first time in his life, he felt that he was a Christian. He was experiencing peace.

We don't put confidence in our feelings, but we surely do enjoy them; and God has made provision for that very human desire.

He has promised us the delightful experience of what He calls an "incomprehensible peace" if we just learn to believe Him enough to thank Him—not for the peace, but for the promises that ultimately produce peace.

Thank-You Therapy is faith in the forgiving grace of God. Thank-You Therapy acts on a promise, not on a feeling.

It accepts a truth regardless of how impossible or implausible it may seem.

It says "Thank You" for a reality without having to secure it with logic or evidence.

QUESTIONS TO REFLECT ON
1. When did you receive Jesus Christ into your life?
2. Have you ever doubted the genuineness of your conversion?
3. Have you ever told anyone?
4. Do you now realize that the good feelings of peace are coupled to the right thinkings of faith? Try believing God and acting on that faith with a simple "Thank You" based on what He says, rather than how you feel.

"Therefore do not be anxious for tomorrow; for tomorrow will care for itself. Each day has enough trouble of its own."
                        Matthew 6:34

CHAPTER SIX

Trusting God for the Unknown

Thank-You Therapy is an act of faith in God's ability to guide His children.

Thank-You Therapy gives thanks for guidance before it is given and for direction before it is determined.

Thank-You Therapy enables us to walk into the unknown and stand in the presence of the unfamiliar because it believes that God is capable of showing His children what He wants them to do and where He wants them to go. It also believes that He is able to make sure they get there.

> I will instruct you and teach you in the way which you should go; I will counsel you with My eye upon you (Psalm 32:8).

●

There's nothing unusual about a cloud accompanying a vast horde of beings as they march across a desert of sun-baked ground. It's raised by the continuous trampling of feet and the rolling of wheels. It often rises to extreme heights and is sometimes visible for miles. It's kicked up *behind* a procession.

We call it dust.

It *is* unusual, though, for a cloud to accompany a vast horde

of beings as they march across a desert of sun-baked ground—
from the *front*. In fact, it's unheard of.

That's just what happened, though, in the Hebrew exodus
from Egypt 3,500 years ago.

We call that God's guidance.

If network television had been in existence in Moses' day, it
would have scooped the industry for all time. Cameramen
could have shot footage of a spectacle that in all history has
never been duplicated.

       Two million people or more—
          Hebrews,
             Egyptians, and
                Nubian slaves of all ages and stages in life
with millions of livestock—
       sheep,
          goats,
             donkeys,
                oxen, and
                cattle
with all their possessions—
       bedrolls,
          rocking chairs,
             cooking utensils
              clothing,
                kitchen tables, and
                washbasins
leaving home. Leaving the only home they had known for 400
years. They were en route to a land they had never seen.

They were led by an 80-year-old man dressed in sheepskin
and carrying a gnarled shepherd's staff.

They were attended by an army of 600,000 Hebrew youngsters dressed in borrowed armor and accompanied by a rickety
cart bearing the mummified remains of a man who'd been dead
nearly 200 years.

They carried no bread for their hunger and no water for
their thirst.

They marched across a parched wasteland without freeways, road signs, of rest stops.

They had no access to minimarts or convenience stores and carried no road maps or credit cards.

But they had a cloud.

Clouds are not common in Egypt,
> or Marah,
>> or Elam,
>>> or Succoth,
>>>> or Rephidim,
>>>>> or even in Sinai.

In this part of the world, the sun shines endlessly and re-lentlessly. Any cloud of any size or shape would be both a source of relief and a cause for interest.

This particular cloud appeared in the land of Goshen just as the procession was about to begin.

It seemed to originate ahead of the vast column as a small whirlwind that danced lightly across the ground just ahead of the group's leader. As it rose upward, it appeared like a col-umn of smoke that spiraled round and round in ever-widening circles. It then billowed across the sky over and above the marchers like a giant sun umbrella.

It protected them from the merciless sun by day, and when it turned into a spiraling, billowing pillar of fire, it warmed them at night.

The cloud's main function was to lead the Hebrews. It led them through an uncharted desert, past hostile enemies, and over barren mountains to a destination none of them had ever seen.

The cloud was God's Old Testament guidance control center.

> And the Lord was going before them in a pillar of cloud by day to lead them on the way, and in a pillar of fire by night to give them light, that He may lead them by day and by night. He did not take away the pillar of cloud by day, nor the pillar of fire by night, from before the people (Exodus 13:21-22).

I have often wished for something just as spectacular to lead me. Some of my most anxious moments have come while seeking direction from the Lord. Even with a promise of guidance as specific and clear as Psalm 32:8, I've still felt anxious.

But then, so did the Hebrews.

Though they had been promised guidance and though the cloud was visible to all, they still became frightened and said:

> It would have been better for us to serve the Egyptians than to die in the wilderness (Exodus 14:12).

That's anxiety.

And though they had been promised adequate provision for their journey, they grumbled and said:

> What shall we drink? (Exodus 15:24)

That's anxiety.

And though they had been promised food for their journey, they were convinced that God was going to let them die of hunger (Exodus 16:3).

That's anxiety, and that anxiety was felt right under the shadow of the cloud.

It's awfully hard to believe God at times, isn't it?

●

When Martha and I were married, we took Psalm 32:8 as a favored and guiding passage of Scripture. At that time, we had no idea what God had in mind for us. We knew we had been called to serve Him. Where, when, how, and to what extent were still unknowns.

And yet, it was right under that cloud of promise that says,
    I will instruct you
        and teach you
            in the way you should go
that I worried about God's guidance.

After the completion of my schooling, I didn't know what to do.

How does a graduate find his first job?

I asked my father-in-law—

"What do I do?"

"Where do I go?"

"To whom do I write?"

"Where do I apply?"

"How do people know that I'm available?"

He gave me the best advice I've ever received regarding God's guidance. He said, "Go into the house and then into your closet. When you have shut the door, talk to your Heavenly Father and ask Him to show you what He wants of you. Your Father has promised to give you direction. If He is not capable of doing that, He isn't worth working for."

I did as he suggested and, just as God had promised, He guided us. Two days after my graduation, I was at work in my first church—full-time.

"I will instruct you and teach you in the way you should go."

That promise applies to every decision in the life of every believer.

Whom do I marry?

Where do I live?

What job should I take?

Where do I go to school?

How many children should we have?

What car do I buy?

A personal God has promised to be involved in the decisions of our lives—not just the major ones, but the seemingly minor ones as well. Just how God does this has been made to seem terribly complex and often contradictory.

Does God guide us mystically and supernaturally, as He did Moses through the wilderness?

Does God guide us through visions, as He did Paul in Acts 16:9?

Does God guide us by circumstance as He did Paul and Silas in Acts 16:16-34?

Does God guide us by His Spirit, as He did Jesus in Mark 1:12-13?

Does God guide us only in our hunger as He did Peter in Acts 10:9-12?

Does God guide us by an angel as He did Cornelius in Acts 10:7-8?

Does God guide us through the church as He did in Acts 13:1-2?

Does God guide us through the constraints of men as He did Jesus in Luke 24:29?

Does God guide us through discussion and even dispute as He did in Acts 15?

Does God guide us through the wisdom of a man as He did in Acts 15:19-21?

Does God guide us through an assembled group of people as He did in Acts 15:22-29?

Does God guide us through the casting of lots as He did in Acts 1:26?

or by fleece (Judges 6–7)

or by donkeys (Numbers 22:28-31)

or by little clouds (1 Kings 18:44)

or by fire (Judges 6:20-23)

or by His voice (Exodus 17:5)

or by fathers-in-law (Exodus 18:13-27)

or by mothers-in-law (Ruth 2:1-23)

or by fathers (Genesis 24:1-8)

or by mothers (Genesis 27:1-25)

or by brothers (Genesis 37:20-36)

or by wives (1 Samuel 19:11-13)

or by friends (1 Samuel 20:1-42)

or by wooden sticks (Exodus 7:10)

or by uncles (Esther 2:20)

or by nieces (Esther 4:15-17)

or

Does He guide us by His Word? (Psalm 119:105)

Some tell us God guides us by our relationships. Others say that God guides us by reason when no specific biblical command is given.

Others tell us to line up counsel, circumstance, and the

Scriptures much like a ship captain would line up the harbor lights as he approaches land, and when they are properly aligned, then proceed.

It's impossible for me to recount every detail of every incident in my life when God has given me guidance. It's also unwise. Some of God's direction in my life has come in bizarre and almost unbelievable ways.

One thing is certain. God has never guided me twice in the same way, and yet God has always guided me.

He has guided me
   through His Word
     by His Spirit
      through friends
       and counselors
       and pastors
       and teachers
      and family
       and impression
        and through peace
        and restlessness
         and He's even used my ego
to get me to do things He's wanted of me.

The things that stand out to me as I recall God's guidance are—

He has never guided me contrary to His revealed Word.

He has always accompanied the right decision with a sense of continuing peace.

My biggest problem has not been in determining the will of God for my life; it has been in waiting for His will to be revealed.

It's in the wait that anxiety is felt, and it's often the influence of mounting anxiety that has caused me to act impulsively.

•

Thank-You Therapy has taught me to relax by giving thanks

for guidance before it is given and for direction before it is determined.

I take Philippians 4:6-7, and I pray about "everything." That includes minor as well as major decisions. Then I thank God that, on the basis of verses like Psalm 32:8 and even Psalm 23:3, He has already promised to guide me.

I stop asking for guidance—I've already asked for that—and I begin simply thanking Him that in His time and in His way He will show me exactly what He wants of me.

Then the peace comes—just as He promised. God's peace sets up a guard over my mind, and I'm able to relax—and wait.

Thank-You Therapy is an act of faith in God's ability to guide His children.

Thank-You Therapy enables us to walk into the unknown and stand in the presence of the unfamiliar because it believes that God is capable of showing His children what He wants them to do and where He wants them to go—and He is able to make sure that we get there.

> I will instruct you and teach you in the way which you should go; I will counsel you with My eye upon you (Psalm 32:8).

One word of caution: *wait!* Wait until you're sure, then move with confidence. God is not the author of confusion.

QUESTIONS TO REFLECT ON
1. Are you presently seeking divine guidance in your life?
2. What is the decision you must make?
3. Have you searched the Scriptures for any mention they might have regarding your quandary?
4. Is there any moral or ethical counsel in Scripture regarding your decision?
5. Do you believe God is wise enough to direct you, interested enough to care, and sovereign enough to employ any means at His disposal to guide you? Then thank Him—in your darkness. He's already promised to give you light.

"Anxiety never releases tomorrow of its problems. It only empties today of its strengths."
—*Corrie ten Boom*

CHAPTER SEVEN
Anxiety about Discipline

Thank-You Therapy thanks God in the midst of a problem—not for the problem, but for the outcome.

Thank-You Therapy believes that the last chapter in every believer's life has already been written. If we know the Scriptures, then we already know what will happen.

Thank-You Therapy thanks God for what it knows in spite of what it sees.

●

One characteristic of authentic Christianity is that it's always thankful. Its continuing thankfulness is grounded in God's ultimate and inevitable triumph.

In a permissive society such as ours, discipline, accountability, or punishment of any kind is risky.

A 16-year-old son had been repeatedly warned against taking his father's car without permission. The father awoke late one night to find both his son and his car missing.

He waited for a reasonable length of time and then called the police to have his son picked up for car theft. He called me with the news of what he had done. "I'm afraid my son will hate me forever, but I had to do something to teach him obedience."

Discipline of any kind in a permissive society is terribly risky.

The anxiety of that parent is matched by the anxiety of the Apostle Paul in 2 Corinthians. It is in that letter that he recounts for us what was possibly his most severe anxiety attack. He wrote:·

"I had no rest for my spirit" (2:13).

"Our flesh had no rest" (7:5).

"We were afflicted . . . [by] fears within" (7:5).

That's anxiety.

His anxiety persisted despite the fact that he was engaged in an extremely successful city-wide evangelistic campaign in Troas (2:12).

The cause of his unrelieved anxiety was the fear that he had overreacted when he had scolded the Corinthian church for its divisiveness, its tolerance of immorality, its rebellion toward and abuses of sacred truth.

He had been quite harsh.

He had referred to them as "babes."

He had identified them as "carnal."

He had rebuked them for "judging."

He had accused them of slander.

He had described them as arrogant.

He had questioned their motives.

He had attacked their power structure.

He had shamed them for their greed.

He had scolded them for being self-seeking.

He had urged extremely painful discipline.

Pastors don't do that sort of thing without expecting some sort of reaction.

Neither do apostles.

Neither do parents.

One of my greatest causes of anxiety is not necessarily the many problems that I'm called upon to face—it's my response to those problems.

When one of my church leaders confessed to me that he was a homosexual, my reaction was violent. I felt I had been

betrayed, deceived, embarrassed—and I told him so. He nearly walked away from me without the help and encouragement
he had requested. It was necessary for me to clear away the
debris left by my reaction before we could attack the problem
that had bound him for 21 years.

I do overreact at times. The result is that people are more
aware of my reaction than they are of the problem.

Jesus has often been accused of overreacting when He
cleansed the temple of its greed. He overthrew the tables of
the money changers, drove out the sheep and oxen, and
scourged those responsible for defiling the place of worship.

My friend feared he had overreacted when he reported his
son to the local sheriff.

Paul was anxious over his reactions to the sins that prompted the writing of 1 Corinthians. He was also anxious over the
response that letter would bring. He said:

> For out of much affliction and anguish of heart I wrote
> to you with many tears; not that you should be made
> sorrowful, but that you might know the love which I
> have especially for you (2 Corinthians 2:4).

That's anxiety.

Discipline always produces anxiety—yet discipline is the
necessary duty of anyone providing leadership, especially spiritual leadership, whether that person is an apostle,
    a pastor,
      a parent, or
        just a friend.
The Scriptures tell us:

> Reprove, rebuke, exhort, with great patience
> (2 Timothy 4:2).

> Brethren, even if a man is caught in any trespass, you
> who are spiritual, restore such a one in a spirit of
> gentleness (Galatians 6:1).

If your brother sins, go and reprove him in private (Matthew 18:15).

Foolishness is bound up in the heart of a child; the rod of discipline will remove it far from him (Proverbs 22:15).

Paul had not overreacted. The problems at Corinth were real. The reports had been accurate. His response was appropriate.

Some Corinthians were offended by his harshness. Rather than discuss the charges, they filed countercharges of their own. They accused him of not keeping his word. They questioned his right to rebuke.

In the Corinthian situation, we have all the components for a full-blown church crisis.

Paul couldn't sleep,
  he couldn't eat,
    he couldn't even preach.

He was rendered helpless by his anxiety.

But in his moment of helplessness, he thanked God. Notice the proximity of two verses in 2 Corinthians 2.

Verse 13 says:

I had no rest in my spirit, not finding Titus my brother.

That's the moment of anxiety when Paul was unable to get a report from Titus as to the conditions in Corinth since the writing of Paul's first letter.

But notice verse 14:

But thanks be to God, who always leads us in His triumph in Christ.

Paul's anxiety gave way to truth. He recognized that he had done what was required of him. The rest was up to God—and God had already promised a victorious outcome.

Paul acknowledged that in spite of how the battle appears to be going, God was going to win the war.

Paul did not place confidence in himself.

Paul did not place his confidence in the Corinthians.

Paul placed his confidence in God.

Discipline always produces anxiety.

There are the anxious moments in preparation when we sift the evidence, search the Scriptures, and pray for the opportune moment, the right word, and the proper spirit.

There are the anxious moments of anticipation when we search our own hearts and examine our own motives.

There is the anxious moment of confrontation when we recognize our own weaknesses but proceed to speak the truth in love.

There is the anxiety of waiting—waiting for the time necessary to allow for a response. We ask ourselves—

Did I do it right?

Did I do it in love?

Will they reject me?

Will they resist me?

Will they reject God? or

Will they repent?

All these thoughts and more caused Paul to have no rest in his spirit. All these thoughts and more made it impossible to continue preaching in Troas—even though preaching was the great love of his life.

It's a terribly anxious moment when a pastor finds it necessary to rebuke a congregation.

It's a terribly anxious moment when a church finds it necessary to discipline a member.

It's a terribly anxious moment when a parent finds it necessary to discipline a child.

●

In the book *Beyond Forgiveness*, I tell the true story of a dear friend and staff member (the man mentioned at the beginning of this chapter) who required discipline for a long-term moral problem. As we worked through Matthew 18:15-20 and then tried to apply it to the problem at hand, we asked ourselves:

Is there any way to avoid public exposure of this sin?

Is it possible to keep this information from the family?

Is it possible to keep our brother in his place of ministry?

Is it possible to restore without censure?

How can we publicly discipline a staff member without hurting the image of the whole church?

How can we lift him up without crippling him further?

How can we preserve the integrity of God and at the same time protect our member?

How can we be true to our Lord and at the same time sensitive to the needs of our brother?

That's anxiety.

Following the public confession and exposure, Martha and I felt terribly anxious. We were concerned about the response of our congregation and its effect on our brother.

The Apostle Paul instructed the Corinthians to withdraw fellowship from the one who was undoubtedly prominent and well liked by his fellow members. His persistent immorality was continuing unchecked (1 Corinthians 5:1-13).

When a pastor—or even an apostle—makes that recommendation, there is always the possibility that the church will withdraw from the pastor—and many have.

Discipline is always a time of anxiety.

A parent's discipline of his child is equally difficult. We fear
the loss of love,
     the loss of respect, even
          the loss of a relationship.

At times fear becomes so great that we withhold discipline. The result is that we often experience the loss of all three.

We disciplined our own children—sometimes severely. Each time that discipline produced its own brand of devastating anxiety. But what a joy to watch our children today—with their children—employing the same discipline, experiencing the same anxiety, but producing the same results.

Paul addressed his anxiety with Thank-You Therapy.

He was not thankful for the problem.

He was not thankful for his response.

He was not even thankful for the people's response.

He was thankful for God's faithfulness.

Obviously he prayed for wisdom when he wrote, and compassion as he chose his words.

Obviously he prayed for repentance to be formed in the hearts of his readers.

But his thankfulness zeroed in on a promise which assured him of an ultimate victory he might not even live long enough to see.

He thanked God for the inevitable triumph that was going to take place in the individual believers' lives and in the church. He thanked God in advance of that triumph.

Sin makes it appear that we have lost a war.

Discipline makes it appear we have lost a war.

In reality we have only lost a battle. Discipline is the proper biblical corrective action that enables us to regroup and that promises us that ultimate triumph belongs to God.

Biblical discipline, when employed in the biblical fashion such as taught in

1 Corinthians 5:1-13,

2 Corinthians 2:5-11,

Matthew 18:15-20, and

Galatians 6:1,

carries with it the guarantee of ultimate triumph. It's one of the necessary elements designed to maintain a pure church and a pure life that can assure us of total victory.

Hebrews 12:5-11 gives the classic exhortation and promise:

And you have forgotten the exhortation which is addressed to you as sons,

"My son, do not regard lightly the discipline of the Lord,

nor faint when you are reproved by Him;
for those whom the Lord loves He disciplines,
And He scourges every son whom He receives."

It is for discipline that you endure; God deals with you as with sons; for what son is there whom his father does not discipline?

But if you are without discipline, of which all have become partakers, then you are illegitimate children and not sons.

Furthermore, we had earthly fathers to discipline us, and we respected them; shall we not much rather be subject to the Father of spirits, and live?

For they disciplined us for a short time as seemed best to them, but He disciplines us for our good, that we may share His holiness.

All discipline for the moment seems not to be joyful, but sorrowful; yet to those who have been trained by it, afterwards it yields the peaceful fruit of righteousness.

Thank-You Therapy, in spite of the pain and anxiety that discipline brings, includes thanksgiving with its prayer for wisdom and love and repentance. It says:

Thank You, Father, that even though all discipline seems not to be joyful but sorrowful, yet to those who have been trained by it, afterwards it yields the peaceful fruit of righteousness.

●

Thank-You Therapy thanks God in the midst of a problem— not for the problem—but for the promised outcome.

Thank-You Therapy thanks God for what it knows in spite of what it sees.

Thank-You Therapy thanks God for triumph even though present circumstances suggest defeat.

QUESTIONS TO REFLECT ON
1. Were you disciplined as a child?
2. How?
3. By whom?
4. Did you feel it was deserved or undeserved?
5. Did you learn from that discipline?
6. Were those lessons negative or positive?
7. Have you seen discipline practiced in a local church?
8. What was the outcome?
9. How, if at all, would you do it differently?

"For this reason I say to you, do not be anxious for your life, as to what you shall eat, or what you shall drink; nor for your body, as to what you shall put on. Is not life more than food, and the body than clothing?"

Matthew 6:25

CHAPTER EIGHT
Anxiety about God's Provision

Thank-You Therapy is not a means of getting what we want; rather, it rests in the promise of God to provide us with what we need.

It is not a plea for provision; it's a grateful response to a promise.

It says "Thank You," not only for what God has given, but for what God is going to give.

•

"I don't know where my next meal is coming from."

"I've lost my job; I'm overage and overqualified."

"It's retirement time and I've no pension or retirement program. Social Security seems like an impossibly small amount to live on."

"My husband was killed in an industrial accident. He had practically no insurance. What will become of me and my children?"

"I'm broke. Black Monday wiped me out."

Anxiety over daily needs is not something confined to Bible times or to present-day Ethiopian drought areas. Anxiety over a need is something very common even in today's affluent America. That anxiety strikes all levels of society.

God's promises are by no means limited to ancient concerns either.

Jesus promised to provide food,
Jesus promised to provide water,
Jesus promised to provide clothing,
Jesus promised to take care of tomorrow.

Matthew 6:25-34

He displayed His ability to do just as He promised by sweetening the bitter waters at Marah (Exodus 15:23-25), catering bread six days each week in the desert (Exodus 16:14-15),

providing quail each evening for a protein snack (Exodus 16:12-13),

again providing water at Horeb (Exodus 17:5-6),

preparing lifetime clothing for the marchers (Deuteronomy 8:4),

feeding Elijah at the brook Cherith (1 Kings 17:2-7), and again at Zarephath (1 Kings 17:8-16),

multiplying the bread and fish to feed 5,000 (Mark 6:32-44), changing water into wine in Cana (John 2:1-11), and borrowing tax money from a fish in Galilee (Matthew 17:27).

It's hard for me to relate to these stories. They're true. There's no doubt about that. But I've never seen

bread dropped from heaven,
water gushing from a barren rock in the desert,
quail just asking to be caught,
clothing that never wears out, or
ravens feeding a man.
I've never watched as 5,000 were fed from a table set just for one, and
I've never seen water changed into wine or a fish cough up coins.

But I have seen God's miraculous providence over and over again in my life and the lives of countless thousands who've learned to trust Him.

Let me tell you some 20th-century stories.

Neither my wife nor I came from wealthy families. We have never inherited a dime or an inch of property. When we married, we were both in school and struggling to pay for our educations. On our wedding day, Dr. Bob Jones, Jr. called long distance to congratulate us and offer each of us a part-time faculty job at $35 per month plus free room and board. We were elated and we accepted.

That's providence.

Martha had no money with which to buy me a matching wedding ring. A local cleaning establishment ruined one of her dresses. They reimbursed her the cost of the garment. She used the money for my ring.

That's providence.

During our first year of marriage we both took a leave of absence from part-time jobs to minister in the West with the American Sunday School Union. We had no income and no money for expenses. God provided gas, food, and shelter daily—as it was needed.

That's providence.

When our first child was born, a truck delivered a clothes dryer to our back door—a clothes dryer provided by an anonymous donor.

That's providence.

When that same child died, a Sunday School class paid for his funeral expenses.

That's providence.

When our son John was born, a truck delivered a crib, high chair, bathinette, and playpen to our door. The giver was again anonymous. (It might have been a raven for all we knew.)

That's providence.

The following day, when food was scarce, friends who owned a produce company dropped by, the back end of their station wagon filled with fresh fruit and vegetables.

That's providence.

When our daughter Kathryn was born, a pharmaceutical salesman offered to provide us with all the prepared baby food we needed.

That's providence.

We lived in rented apartments or church-provided parsonages during our early ministry. Cash savings or home equities were both foreign to us. When the opportunity came to buy our first home, no down payment was available. Our realtor advanced us part of the money. A friend supplied the rest.

That's providence.

That equity, which represents our savings, has grown appreciably. We will never own a home, but we have sufficient equity to enable us to live comfortably.

That's providence.

College tuition for both our children always seemed remote and impossible. Though I purchased insurance policies designed to mature at the appropriate time, I was always forced to draw from them or cash them in when money was scarce. When John graduated from high school, a friend of mine in the appliance business paid John's first year's tuition with an unexpected bonus he'd received. Another friend helped finish John's college tuition. Another paid much of his seminary fees.

That's providence.

Kathy's tuition was provided through unexpected scholarships and gifts. Between the two children, they secured 13 years of graduate work.

That's providence.

We've never owned a beach cottage or a mountain cabin. Vacations were always a clumsy time due to lack of funds. Yet each summer friends have offered us accommodations, luxurious at times, at no expense to us.

That's providence.

During one very weary summer, friends invited us to spend 10 wonderful days in Hawaii with them—at their expense.

That's providence.

In the year of the moon landing, 1969, I landed in Pusan, South Korea for a month of evangelistic meetings and pastors conferences. I was in a state of exhaustion when I left for the Orient. Our church was apprehensive, but prayerful.

Thirty-one days and 20,000 souls later I began my long

trip home. I stood in the Pusan airport surrounded by my new friends, silently praying that I wouldn't collapse from weariness.

A stranger appeared, ushered me and my host into the VIP lounge, and invited me to lie down. The same stranger sat beside me as we flew to Seoul. He accompanied me off the plane. He saw my large, flimsy suitcase as it was dropped to the tarmac, spilling its contents in all directions. He took my arm, told me not to worry, as with a snap of his fingers, he recruited a small army of airport personnel to gather up my belongings.

I worried.

I asked him where I could buy a new case.

He said, "Don't worry."

I worried.

I asked him where to go to find my suitcase.

He said, "Don't worry."

I worried.

I asked him about going through customs.

He said, "Don't worry."

I worried.

He escorted me to another VIP lounge, sat with me while I rested, and then finally walked with me to my plane.

I asked him about my luggage.

He said, "Don't worry."

I worried—until he helped me into my seat aboard the aircraft. He then smiled, prayed with me, handed me his business card, and left. His card introduced him to me as "Chief of Customs, Republic of South Korea." My new suitcase, with all its contents neatly packed inside, arrived safely with me in Japan.

That's providence.

The airliner from Seoul to Japan was full. Every seat was taken—except the two alongside me. The cabin attendant smiled, raised the armrests in the adjoining seats, provided some pillows and a blanket, and tucked me in for the flight.

That's providence.

Flying from Seoul to Tokyo aboard that Japan Air Lines flight, I ministered to a Japanese woman suffering from an embolism to the brain. Doctors say that I saved her life. Japan Air Lines, in their gratitude, thanked me, sent me a gift, and provided luxurious (and restful) accommodations in Tokyo during my 26-hour layover.

That's providence.

They also made sure that my accommodations from Tokyo to Vancouver, British Columbia were adequate for me to rest. I slept all the way.

That's providence.

The Canadian Pacific flight to Vancouver was delayed. I was rushed through customs but arrived at the gate too late. I was denied boarding. This was especially critical to me since Martha was to meet me in Los Angeles. We had planned to celebrate our 20th anniversary together.

But I had another problem. Two one-dollar bills were all I had left in my billfold. That's not much for a celebration in a big city.

I caught another flight three hours later and *just happened* to read the information about denied boarding. I qualified. Martha met me at the terminal, United Airlines graciously paid me $79 cash as a "denied boarding refund," and we spent a delightful anniversary celebration in plush accommodations in Los Angeles.

That's providence.

We arrived back home in Fresno in time for the funeral of a dear friend, whose death had seemed imminent five weeks before.

That's providence.

When Martha was invited to develop the speech department at Multnomah School of the Bible in Portland, we needed a second car. At that time a second car was preposterous and unthinkable. Within hours of the invitation, a builder in the church approached me and said, "I've got an old Chevy that I'm not using. Do you know anyone who needs it?"

That's providence.

We've never pastored a church that made any provision for retirement. As I approached my 62nd birthday, I visited the Social Security office and was stunned at being told how much was available. Retirement was impossible—but retirement was necessary. Thirty-eight years of pastoring had taken its toll. I was tired.

One week after announcing retirement from our church in Rockford, Illinois, the invitation came to become pastor to a thousand churches and missionaries all over the world. As Minister-at-Large for the Conservative Baptist Association of America, I'm busy traveling, preaching, and counseling—at a pace I can maintain—and we are enjoying a fulfillment in ministry that we had never dreamed possible.

That's providence.

The only major stress of our extensive nonstop flight schedule (in which we have accrued more than 100,000 miles in just eight months) was that of boarding, stowing luggage, and crowding into filled coach cabins. This too was relieved when United Airlines unexpectedly mailed me a Premier Frequent Flyers Pass that has allowed for upgrading to first class and has taken all the hassle out of my twice-weekly flights.

That's providence.

The 1st-century Scriptures are filled with 20th-century promises. God seldom uses ravens and fish and clouds and stones to meet our needs today. He could if He had to, but He uses whatever resources are available to meet those daily needs.

The promises are still valid—

> And my God shall supply all your needs according to His riches in glory in Christ Jesus (Philippians 4:19).

> The Lord is my shepherd, I shall not want (Psalm 23:1).

> The young lions do lack and suffer hunger; but they who seek the Lord shall not be in want of any good thing (Psalm 34:10).

But seek first His kingdom and His righteousness; and all these things shall be added to you (Matthew 6:33).

For the Lord God is a sun and a shield; the Lord gives grace and glory; no good thing will He withhold from those who walk uprightly (Psalm 84:11).

People ask me, "Do these promises mean that I need not make provision for my tomorrows?"

They don't mean that to me. I make whatever preparations I can, but when I'm unable to do anymore, then God's promises become my source of peace.

●

Thank-You Therapy is not a means of getting what we want; rather, it rests in God's promise to provide us what we need.

It's not a plea for provision; it's a response to a promise.

It says, "Thank You," not only for what God has given, but for what God is going to give.

It relaxes in the promises of the sustaining grace of God and enjoys peace as it trusts in His providence.

It says, "Thank You, Father, that You're going to meet my needs today."

QUESTIONS TO REFLECT ON
1. What is the most nagging concern you face daily as you think of your needs or your family's needs?
2. How many times has this worry ballooned into a full-scale crisis?
3. Have you ever taken time to reflect on God's providence in your life?
4. Have you shared it with others?
5. Have you told it to your children? (In Deuteronomy 31:13, Moses instructed the Israelites to tell their children of God's provision in their lives: "And their children, who have not known, will hear and learn to fear the Lord your God, as long as you live.")

*"And which of you by being anx-
ious can add a single cubit to
his life's span? If then you cannot do even a very little thing,
why are you anxious about other
matters?"*

Luke 12:25-26

CHAPTER NINE
Anxiety about God's Timing

Thank-You Therapy is not designed to change God's timetable or speed up the divine program. It enables me to adjust my schedule to His.

It does not grant my wishes more quickly, but enables me to wait.

It will not push me to the head of the line, but will help me to be patient.

●

For impatient people like me, timing is always a crucial problem. If I'm not early, I consider myself late.

I move my watch hands ahead to be prompt. I waken hours before I need to in order to arrive ahead of time. I'll wait for hours in preference to being one minute late.

I want everything done by yesterday. If that's impossible, TODAY then becomes a necessary but totally unacceptable alternative.

I stopped at a local deli recently for a quick sandwich. Four people were in line ahead of me. I hate lines. I'd rather waste an hour searching for a line-free eating establishment than to spend 15 minutes waiting for a table.

As I waited,

I fidgeted,
   I sighed,
      I groaned,
I looked at my watch repeatedly and wondered how humans could be so slow.

I was about to leave in disgust when I noticed a small sign strategically placed above the cash register. It read:

RELAX, GOD'S IN CONTROL.

It took a few moments, but finally I smiled and said, "Thank You, Father."

For one who wants everything accomplished immediately, it's hard to fully comprehend the biblical "one day with God is as a thousand years, and a thousand years as one day." A day often seems like a thousand years, but I have difficulty understanding how a thousand years could be as a day. But that's what it says.

God lives in eternity, and eternity has no time clocks.
There is no yesterday,
   no today, and
      no tomorrow.
There is no morning,
   no noon, and
      no night.
There is no dawn and no dusk
There is no sunrise and no sunset.
There will be no Big Bens, no sundials, and no calendars. My Omega will become a collector's item—even Rolex will be out of business.

Measuring time on earth is somewhat like watching the Tournament of Roses Parade from curbside. We see it in segments. It has a beginning, a continuance, and an ending.

God's perspective is totally different. He looks down upon the entire event from His Goodyear blimp and sees it all at once.

With God, what will happen has happened,

what has happened is still happening, and
  what is happening is already past.
Eternity removes all the anxiety from Time.

God can see the total picture at one glance and then drop
any event He wishes into any time slot He desires. Since He
can already see my past, present, and future, He can place any
event of my lifetime into the most appropriate time slot and
cause it to happen at just the right moment.

The problem is, the "right moment" seems to always take
longer than we think it should. In our youth, time never moved
fast enough. In our old age, we attempt by any means possible
to slow it down.

●

The Apostle Paul used a little phrase in Galatians 4:4 to
describe the precision God employs whenever He controls an
event. The words *in the fullness of time* are used to pinpoint to
the microsecond the moment Jesus was born in the Judean
town of Bethlehem.

The phrase suggests that time accumulates like coffee in a
cup, and when the coffee level reaches the brim—when not
one more drop can be added—when it's about to spill over the
sides—it's then that time is full.

God's preplanned events occur
  when every prophetic utterance has been fulfilled,
    when every circumstance has transpired,
      when every personality is in his precise place,
        when all has happened that needs to happen,
          when God's sovereignty will receive the great-
          est visibility,
            when God's purpose will acquire the greatest
            benefit, and
              when we will sense the greatest blessing.

Yes, the birth of Jesus is a classic illustration of God's sense
of timing. Galatians 4:4 says,

But when the fullness of time came, God sent forth
His Son, born of a woman, born under the Law.

At just the right moment, Jesus came.

That was 4,000 years after the first promise was made.

That was 2,000 years after Abraham began waiting for Him.

That was 1,500 years after Moses began telling God's people that Jesus would come.

That was 1,000 years after David began looking for a qualified king to sit on his throne.

That was 700 years after Isaiah,

600 years after Jeremiah,

500 years after Daniel,

and 400 years after Malachi—

a long time to wait for the fulfillment of a promise. And yet, each of them lived on the tiptoe of expectancy, fully believing he'd see God's promised deliverer.

None of them saw Him.

None of them stopped hoping.

They believed,

    they waited, and

        they died without having received what was promised.

All of them prayed with thanksgiving—thanking God in advance for what had not yet happened.

They wondered, as do we, why didn't God act sooner?

Why didn't God send Jesus sooner?

Why didn't these earlier generations of humanity have the benefit of His incarnation and His atonement?

Why wasn't a spiritual crisis-center established immediately just outside the Garden of Eden?

Why wasn't a spiritual advanced life-support system made available when man first experienced spiritual death?

Why did God allow at least 4,000 years to pass as the world sunk deeper and deeper into its ignorance and unbelief?

I have asked the same question as it relates to other necessities in our lives.

●

On August 1, 1944, Manuel L. Quezon, President of the Philippines, died in Saranac Lake, a vacation resort for tuberculosis patients in upstate New York. He had been suffering from the disease for many years.

That same year streptomycin was developed and within a few months it was hailed as the long-awaited miracle drug for tuberculosis. Within five years the Saranac Lake sanitorium was closed for lack of patients.

Why wasn't streptomycin discovered sooner?

In 1934 two youngsters in Bremerton, Washington suffered for months the painful agonies and debilitation of infantile paralysis or polio. One died; the other lived. I was that one survivor.

Why was it that the Salk vaccine was discovered in 1955 and not 1925?

In 1953 our son Jimmy died at Doernbecher Children's Hospital of a congenital heart condition. We were told that Dr. Starr was sorry, but nothing could be done. "Someday," he said, "we'll be able to solve the problem, even to the replacing of the defective heart with another."

Today heart transplants are routine surgical procedures for the same doctor who admitted his helplessness 35 years earlier.

But why not sooner?

Have you ever questioned God's timing?

We have all waited
     and waited
          and waited; and some are still waiting for God to do something that's deeply wanted.

God has an uncanny sense of timing. The birth of Jesus is a lasting tribute to His precision.

He waited until all the necessary prophetic utterances had been made,
     and until Isaiah had announced His birthplace
          and given Him some special names,
               until Jeremiah had described His righteous kingdom.
He didn't send His Son until the whole story had been told—in advance.

He waited until the Old Testament Scriptures, lost during the Babylonian Captivity, had been found, restored completely, and translated into Greek.

He waited until Greece had united all of civilization into one world.

He waited until Roman roads made all parts of the world accessible.

He waited until the Jews were dispersed among all nations.

He waited until the world was at peace.

He waited until mankind was convinced of its helplessness.

He waited until the world was ready—until *He* was ready.

He waited until there were no confusing sounds—no distracting announcements—until the world was silent.

Mary wasn't distracted.

The shepherds weren't watching Monday night football.

The wise men were expectant.

In the precise moment of the world's greatest darkness and silence,

the light shone,

the angel spoke, and

Jesus came.

That's God's perfect timing.

I would have wanted it sooner. You probably would have wanted it sooner.

Anything worth waiting for is worth waiting for.

One of our greatest problems is that of facing up to the inexorable fact that God does not hurry to give us what we need in the development of our Christian life.

We all want instant maturity, but maturity does not come instantly. It takes time. Miles Sanford reminds us of the student who asked the president of his school whether he could not take a shorter course than the one prescribed. "Oh yes," replied the president, "but then it depends upon what you want to be. When God wants to make an oak, He takes a hundred years, but when He wants to make a squash, He takes six months" (*Principles of Spiritual Growth*, Back to the Bible, 1987, p. 12).

In our impatience we have settled for something less than God's best for our lives. We have, at times, hurried the birth of God's perfect provision until we have aborted His offspring and produced nothing but a hideous replica of something originally designed to be perfect.

What's worth waiting for is worth waiting for.

●

Thank-You Therapy is the best solution I have found for the problem of my impatience. I have learned to thank God for
His sovereign control of time and eternity,
His infinite wisdom that controls His decisions, and
His perfect timing.
Thank-You Therapy says, "Thank You, Father, not just for what You've done, but for what You're going to do."

It does not change God's timetable or speed up the divine program. It enables me to wait.

QUESTIONS TO REFLECT ON
1. Is there some event for which you're anxiously waiting?
2. What is it?
3. When do you want it to happen?
4. Why?
5. Why hasn't it happened?
6. Why do you think God has not allowed it to happen yet?
7. Are there things that you know might be causing the delay?
8. What are you doing about them?

"For we do not know how to pray as we should, but the Spirit Himself intercedes for us with groanings too deep for words."
Romans 8:26

CHAPTER TEN
Anxiety about Prayer

Thank-You Therapy believes in prayer.

It accepts prayer as not only a Christian privilege, but also as a Christian responsibility.

It places its confidence, however, not in the act of prayer, but in the God who
> solicits prayer,
>> hears prayer, and
>>> answers prayer.

Thank-You Therapy likewise recognizes that we don't always know just how to pray.

It admits to
> confused thinking,
>> carnal desires, and even
>>> garbled messages.

But it prays anyway.

●

Thank-You Therapy believes in a Go-Between God who is able to translate our confusion and even rearrange our requests. Our Go-Between God, the Holy Spirit, is even able to take the prayer that cannot be spoken, frame it into words, and relay it to our listening Heavenly Father.

Many times I've been unable to pray—too weary, too confused, or too heavyhearted.

My praying consisted of groans that emitted from a struggling spirit, or sighs that lifted from a burdened soul. At times my prayer has consisted of only two words, just

Dear Father.

That prayer didn't know where to go or what to ask. It just called out the only words it could speak and then settled back into a troubled mind and stayed there.

When I was hospitalized for severe depression, my prayer life was limited to those two words.

I didn't want to pray.

I didn't know what to ask.

I didn't even know what I wanted.

The human mind was bewildered and confused by all sorts of strange ideas and baffling thoughts, and it was unable to frame a coherent request.

One moment I would pray to die. The next moment I would pray to live.

I would ask for healing, and then I would pray for the strength to run.

Should I resign from my pastorate, or should I not resign? If I didn't resign, how could I carry on? If I did resign, what would I do?

As much as I needed to pray, I could not pray.

It was during those never-ending weeks that I learned the meaning of the word *abide.* I realized that I really didn't need to say anything to God—nor did I need to listen for God to say anything to me. It was a time when, as my wife put it, I just figuratively climbed up into my Lord's lap, leaned my head on His shoulder, and rested.

As time passed, "Dear Father" extended itself to include the words, "Thank You."

Thank-You Therapy believes that even though God asks us to pray without ceasing, there are those times that the jumbled concerns of our hearts can never quite be framed into coherent speech.

Thank-You Therapy also recognizes that the anxiety of a particular circumstance can even be heightened by an inability to know how to pray.

Specific praying in any given crisis is difficult because none of us can foresee the future.

●

As I am writing this chapter, we have just been pushed into another difficult experience.

My mother, who is 91 years old, and who has always been
    independent,
      self-sufficient,
        resourceful, and
          energetic,
now needs nursing home or residential care.

She has been widowed for 37 years. During all that time, and before, she has worked and managed to supplement a very meager Social Security income.

Four of us call her "Mother."

Ten of us call her "Grandmother."

Twenty-five of us call her "Great-Grandmother."

Five more call her "Great-Great-Grandmother."

More than 700 people scattered all over the world affectionately call her "Mom" from the 25 years she house-mothered at the University of Oregon, Oregon State University, and Linfield College.

Recently she was featured in Portland's daily newspaper, *The Oregonian,* and on NBC Television as "Grandma Helen," that remarkable little 90-year-old woman who rides the bus daily to the Westminster Presbyterian Church to play "Grandma." There she works 4 hours each day with 13 children as a foster grandparent for the Multnomah County Child Development Center.

And then she fell.

It was at a Sunday School class picnic. She lost her balance, fractured a small cervical bone, and finally had to accept the fact that her work career was finished.

What eventually happens to all the elderly has happened to "Grandma Helen." Unable to care for herself, and having a family that is financially unable to provide her the $1,000–$1,500 per month facility she deserves, she finds herself at the mercy of a society that cares—but only a little.

I called to secure a list of residential care facilities that accept Medicaid patients and was told—

"If you're going to get old, you'd better be rich; if you're not rich, you'd better be nice."

I was also told,

"No, it's illegal to supplement her Social Security and Medicaid. She either goes on Medicaid, which will allow her only minimal funds, or she, or the family, pays for her care privately."

None of us has sufficient funds. She presently lives in subsidized housing for $67.50 per month and has no savings to fall back on.

What do we do?

All of us strongly resist placing her in any of the facilities that were available to her.

She deserves better.

How do we pray?

The future is an unknown to us at this time. We don't know what to pray for—

an adequate facility?

for how long?

for how much?

with what sort of care?

This is where Thank-You Therapy comes in. Thank-You Therapy doesn't know what specifics to place before God, so it's forced to say,

Father, thank You that You know Mother. You know us—You know our dilemma and You already know the solution to our problem. Thank You that You will show us what to do and when to do it, and that You will provide for these needs as You promised.

At present, that's not the solution to our problem, but that's God's provision for our anxiety.

●

Specific praying in a given crisis can be difficult because we don't always know what is best for us.

The Apostle Paul at one time was convinced that healing was best for him. He prayed three times to be rid of his "thorn in the flesh," as he called it.

Healing, he reasoned, would enable him to have a more effective and energetic ministry. Good health would seem to be a reasonable request for a man whose travels would carry him more than 10,000 miles. It would also seem reasonable to assume that robust health would be a far better testimonial to the God of power than a life of limiting weakness.

He was wrong.

Paul failed to take into account that divine strength is best evidenced in the presence of human. weakness. His affliction became a greater provision for ministry than his good health.

He prayed for healing until he acknowledged that his prayer was faulty. Finally he said,

> Therefore, I am well content with weaknesses . . . for when I am weak, then I am strong (2 Corinthians 12:10).

●

I love to hear my grandchildren pray. They pray with faith, fervor, and innocence. I must admit, though, that sometimes their prayers are difficult to translate and possibly even more difficult to answer.

At Christmastime both Jamie and Jeff offered to pray at the breakfast table.

Jamie prayed:

"Dear Jesus, thank You for this food. We love You. Please let it snow today. In Jesus' name, Amen."

Jeff prayed:

"Dear Jesus, thank You for this food. We love You.
Please let it be warm today."

It may seem that those two juvenile prayers canceled each
other out—and probably would have if only human ears had
been listening. But each of those brief sentences was filtered
through the human spirit to the Holy Spirit, who is able to take
human wishes and translate them into heavenly language and
make them intelligible to God's listening ears.

(Incidentally, it was clear and warm that day. The snow-
flakes waited to fall until after dark.)

•

I'm often called to sit with anxious families as they watch the
approaching death of a loved one. Recently one such family
joined hands and prayed.

One grandchild prayed,

"Father, please don't let Grandpa die."

Another prayed,

"Father, please, please take Grandpa home to heaven
soon so he doesn't have to suffer."

Even Jesus struggled to reconcile His human wishes with
His Father's will when He said,

"Father, if Thou art willing, remove this cup from Me"
(Luke 22:42).

That's the Son of God displaying very human resistance to
the prospect of suffering and death.

That's the sinless One recoiling from the inevitable moment
when He was to become sin.

That's God the Son asking God the Father to do something
that He could not and would not do.

That's humanity wishing for something that could not
happen.

We do not always know what's best for us—nor are we able
to foresee the future.

In each instance—not knowing the future and not knowing
what's best for us—we can relax in thanksgiving because we
do know that our Go-Between God not only knows what we

need, but He also prays for that need when we cannot.

And we say—

"Thank You, Father, for taking my jumbled thoughts and my confused thinking and for gently and gradually revealing to me what Your plan has been all along."

QUESTIONS TO REFLECT ON

1. What crisis are you facing about which you're confused in knowing exactly how to pray?
2. What do you want to happen?
3. What are the other options?
4. Do you sense God's peace in the request that you're presently making?
5. Are you able to say, as Jesus said in His confusion, "Yet not My will, but Thine be done"? (Luke 22:42)

The ultimate anxiety is death—but divine provision has even been made for that.

"Since then the children share in flesh and blood, He Himself [Christ] likewise also took the same, that through death He might render powerless him who had the power of death, that is, the devil; and might deliver those who through fear of death were subject to slavery all their lives."

Hebrews 2:14-15

CHAPTER ELEVEN
Anxiety about Death

Thank-You Therapy is not intended to eliminate the inevitable. It's not even designed to delay it.

Thank-You Therapy acknowledges death, not as an end, but as a beginning—not as a defeat, but as a victory.

Thank-You Therapy gives eternal perspective to life's most anxious moment.

Thank-You Therapy enables us to face death, discuss it, and even be thankful for it.

●

"I'm going to die soon;
  I know how,
    I know when, and
      I know where.

"My death is going to involve
    prolonged anguish,
      indescribable loneliness, and
        unbelievable humiliation.

"It's going to tax My endurance,
    test My faith, and

crush My spirit.

"I'm going to be
   killed by the people I love,
     taunted by the ones I helped, and
      deserted by the Father I trust.

"I'm going to die."

These are some of the thoughts Jesus repeatedly expressed as He approached the shame and pain of Calvary.

Repeatedly, as the time of death drew near, He said:

> We are going up to Jerusalem, and the Son of Man will be delivered to the chief priests and the scribes; and they will condemn Him to death, and will deliver Him to the Gentiles. And they will mock Him and spit upon Him, and scourge Him, and kill Him, and three days later He will rise again (Mark 10:33-34).

Jesus' announcement was not a premonition, but a prophecy.

It was not a feeling, but a fact.

He was not being psychic—He was being God.

He knew He was going to die.
   He knew how,
     He knew when, and
      He knew where.

He knew that in the very near future, He would experience—
   the betrayal of Judas,
     the denial of Peter,
      the desertion of His disciples,
       the travail of His soul,
        the withdrawal of His Father, and
        the crucifixion of His body.

Four times the Gospel writers pull back the curtain of mystery that veiled the humanity of the God-Man to let us know just how He felt—

> Mark tells us that He "began to be very distressed and troubled" (Mark 14:33).
>
> John tells us that "He became troubled in spirit" (John 13:21).
>
> Jesus Himself told us that His "soul has become troubled" (John 12:27).
>
> And again He said, "My soul is deeply grieved to the point of death" (Mark 14:34).

That's anxiety.

That's the upheaval of all human emotions.

That's the distress of the human spirit.

That's the anguish of heart and mind as it resists life's greatest insult and heaven's ultimate trauma.

That's God resisting humanity's biggest flaw.

That's God struggling against earth's severest pain.

That's God moving inexorably toward His own painfully humiliating demise.

That's God about to die.

That's anxiety.

Even Jesus couldn't escape the heartrending turbulence of the anxiety of dying.

●

Death produces so much human anxiety that we even refuse to talk about it.

As with most unsolvable problems, we deal with it in the most irrational manner, refusing to discuss it and think about it—even to the point of denying its very reality.

My father lived with terminal cancer for more than three years. During that time we never spoke of death. We talked about everything else—

> the weather,
> > the local baseball team,
> > > the church,
> > > > the food,
> > > > > the nurses and
> > > > > > the doctors,

our aches and pains, and
when to crank up and
crank down the bed.

We never talked about death.

I watched his body waste away to less than 70 pounds. I lifted him and turned him every 30 minutes when he was home. I saw the gradual increases in pain medication. I watched his eyes as they lost their luster. I strained more and more to hear a voice that was losing its energy. I felt his fingers weaken as they held my hand. I watched as he required more care and craved less nourishment. The signs of approaching death were obvious—but were never mentioned.

That's anxiety. That response is very human.

But Jesus *did* talk about it—and when He did, Peter rebuked Him (Mark 8:32) and James and John ignored Him (Mark 10:33-35).

That too is anxiety.

But Jesus still talked about it, and talking about death can in itself be very therapeutic.

Jesus prayed about it. He also employed Thank-You Therapy. His Thank-You was the humble submission of a troubled soul to the infinite wisdom of His sovereign Father.

His Thank-You Therapy took place in a borrowed guest-chamber on the Thursday evening prior to His death. Jesus had met with His disciples to celebrate the Passover. It was traditional to remember God's miraculous deliverance of the Hebrews from their bondage in Egypt by first killing a lamb in the afternoon and then eating together after sundown.

The lamb was killed and roasted in the prescribed manner and then eaten as the 13 men reclined around the table in what has come to be known as the Upper Room.

During the meal, Jesus departed from the 1,500-year-old tradition and established a new one. He took one of the unleavened cakes prescribed for the meal and blessed it.

"This is My body," He said. He then took one of the four cups used to celebrate the Passover, passed it among them, and said, "This is My blood of the covenant, which is to be shed on behalf of many. Truly I say to you I shall never again drink of the fruit of the vine until that day when I drink it new in the kingdom of God" (Mark 14:22-25).

Prior to that moment He had paused, looked carefully into the cup, studied its contents, and said, "Thank You, Father . . ." (Mark 14:23).

Jesus was not naive concerning what was about to happen.

Unlike us, He was not moving into the experience of death in ignorance.

When He picked up that little unleavened biscuit and broke a piece from it, then announced that it symbolized His body freely given to all mankind, He knew exactly what was about to happen.

He knew that soon a Roman soldier would strip Him of the dignity of clothing, tie His hands to an upright post, then take a whip and begin flogging Him.

His back, buttocks, and legs would be beaten, either by two soldiers or by one who alternated positions, until He was weakened to a state just short of collapse or death.

He knew that the little iron balls and the jagged sheep bones attached to the ends of the whip would cut through the skin and produce quivering ribbons of flayed flesh.

He knew all this, and yet He gave thanks.

He knew that a robe would be rudely thrown over His torn and bleeding shoulders and that a staff would be shoved into His right hand, and thorns pushed through the flesh on His head.

Yet He gave thanks.

He knew that in that weakened condition He would be forced to carry His own 300-pound cross from the flogging post to the place of crucifixion.

He knew He would be roughly thrown to the ground and that five- to seven-inch iron spikes, squared at the point, would be driven through His wrists and His feet.

He knew, and yet He gave thanks.

He knew as He looked at that small unassuming piece of unleavened bread, which was to become symbolic of His body, that flies and other insects would soon burrow into those open wounds. They would crawl into His eyes and ears and nose and that He would be helpless to prevent it.

He knew that each wound inflicted upon Him was intended to produce intense agony. When He would be thrown to the ground, His wounds would be torn open again and would become contaminated with dirt.

He knew that the driven spike would crush the large nerves in His wrists and send excruciating bolts of fiery pain into both arms.

He knew that while He was hanging with arms outstretched on that cross, He wouldn't be able to breathe without pushing up with His already lacerated feet and pulling with His pain-racked wrists. He knew that each breath would cause Him to painfully scrape His scourged back against the crude and splintered wood that held Him.

He knew, and yet He gave thanks.

He knew about the taunts, the threats. He knew about the spear. He even knew who would thrust it into His side and when and just how it would feel.

He knew, and yet He gave thanks.

As He looked into the red liquid that sat in the Passover cup, He knew just how and when and where each drop of life-sustaining blood would flow from His torn veins and arteries. He could feel it in advance, tickling His sensitive flesh as it coursed down from His wounded head, through His eyes, over His nose and mouth and chin.

He could see His life as it was being poured out of His body, and dumped on the dry, parched ground to form patches of reddish-brown mud.

He knew it, He felt it, He saw it in advance, and He gave thanks anyway.

His prayer of thanksgiving was not intended to eliminate the inevitable.

It was not even designed to delay it.

For what, then, could Jesus be thankful?

Jesus knew that His death was part of a plan—part of *the*

plan that could never be accomplished apart from it. When He
began talking about His death to His disciples, He said,

"I *must* suffer,
be rejected, and
be killed" (Mark 8:31).

He knew that after His death, God would not only raise Him
up but would "also exalt Him, and bestow on Him the name
which is above every name, that at the name of Jesus every
knee should bow, of those who are in heaven and on earth,
and under the earth" (Philippians 2:9-10).

He knew even more. In thanking the Father, He was also
envisioning a sin-imprisoned world with all of its helpless cap-
tives, the restoration of an entire universe, and the future joy
of presenting renewed, regenerated, redeemed peoples from
every nation on earth as a gift to His Father.

This was why He could say, "Thank You, Father."

•

Has it ever occurred to you there are aspects of your death
for which you can be thankful?

For instance—

Thank You, Father, that death is part of the plan. We
can never experience the complete and total release
from sin apart from it.

Thank You, Father, for the promise of a resurrec-
tion—that my body is going to be literally raised out of
the grave, that I'm going to be with Christ forever
(1 Thessalonians 4:13-18).

Thank You, Father, that You have already prepared a
place for me (John 14:1-2), that You designed it (Hebrews 11:10), that You've even described it (Revelation 21—22), and that eventually it will be my eternal
home.

Thank-You Therapy is not intended to eliminate the
inevitable.

It isn't even designed to delay it.

Thank-You Therapy enables us to face death, discuss it, accept it, and even be thankful for it.

Thank-You Therapy sees death, not as an end, but as a beginning; not as a defeat, but as a victory.

Thank-You Therapy gives eternal perspective to life's most anxious moment and does exactly as God has promised in Philippians 4:6-7: It causes us to be at peace.

QUESTIONS TO REFLECT ON

1. How and when do you think you might die? (Oh yes, you do have the slightest idea—you've thought about it—you just haven't talked with anyone about it.)
2. Have you talked openly with your family about the realities of death?
3. Have you listed things about death for which you can be thankful?
4. Have you shared those things with your loved ones?

"Search me, O God, and know my heart, try me and know my anxious thoughts; and see if there be any hurtful way in me."
Psalm 139:23-24

CHAPTER TWELVE
Friendly Anxiety

Anxiety can sometimes be a friend.

It can be the caution light that warns us of approaching danger.

It can be the spiritual sonar that bounces signals off another person's soul to indicate problems in a relationship.

It can be the Holy Spirit's early-warning device to spotlight a hidden sin or a careless decision.

It can be God's way of telling us that things are not right— even that we are not right.

It can drive us to a doctor or a counselor. It can also point us to God.

Thank-You Therapy responds to an anxiety before its cause is known and soothes it before its cure has even been discovered.

●

King David gives us an example of "friendly" anxiety.

David's early conquests in Israel made him a hero in the eyes of his people, but not in the eyes of his king. As David's popularity rose, Saul's jealousy increased.

In gratitude for his conquests, King Saul gave him a seat at his table and

a place in his family.
Saul's son gave him his armor;
Saul's daughter gave her hand in marriage;
Israel's women gave their praise, and
all Israel gave David their hearts (1 Samuel
17–19).
The jealous king became fearful of his declining popularity
and anxious for his throne.
He sent David to war to die.
He commanded Jonathan to kill him.
He sent spies to find him and
soldiers to capture him.
He threw spears to pierce him.
He even slew 85 priests, along
with their families, for hiding him (1 Samuel 17–19).
David fled to the wilderness,
the mountains,
the strongholds,
his enemies,
his friends,
the caves, and
finally to Engedi.
He hid,
he ran,
he fought,
he recruited his own army,
he scribbled on the walls, and even
dribbled on the floor like a mad man (1 Samuel 20–24).
David was fearful for his life. He was also anxious to know
the reason for his king's anger.
Why was he so hated?
What had he done wrong?
Was there a sin he hadn't acknowledged?
Why was his life in such turmoil?
Anxiety was causing him to search his past, his present, his

heart, and his mind. He brought his whole life under divine scrutiny.

In the seventh Psalm, his mouth speaks the words that are on his heart:

> O Lord my God, in Thee I have taken refuge;
> save me from all those who pursue me and deliver me,
> lest he tear my soul like a lion,
> dragging me away, while there is none to deliver.

That's anxiety.
He continues,

> O Lord my God, if I have done this,
> if there is injustice in my lands,
> if I have rewarded evil to my friend,
> or have plundered him who without cause was my adversary,
> let the enemy pursue my soul and overtake it;
> and let him trample my life down to the ground (Psalm 7:1-5).

That's anxiety.
Finally he said,

> Search me, O God, and know my heart;
> try me and know my anxious thoughts;
> and see if there be any hurtful way in me,
> and lead me in the everlasting way (Psalm 139:23-24).

David did not know what he'd done.
David *did* know that it was possible to sin without knowing it. He knew that it was possible to do wrong, thinking it was right—to do evil, thinking it was good. David knew that it was possible to do something with the full approval of his mind, but without the full approval of his God.
David did know that

the heart is more deceitful than all else and is desper-
ately sick (Jeremiah 17:9).

Sin can be terribly deceptive.
Satan can be awesomely subtle.
David remembered that man's first encounter with the ene-
my was lost due to deception (Genesis 3).

●

I spoke with an airline pilot who had recently found Christ.
He told me that his story was a fairly common one in the
industry. A pilot, with years of experienced flying, 20 years of
marriage, 3 kids, a great wife, and a nice home, becomes
bored with it all. He falls in love with "one of the girls in the
back."
His wife tells him it's wrong,
  his kids tell him it's wrong,
    his pastor tells him it's wrong,
      his friends tell him it's wrong—but, he said,
        "Everyone saw it but me."
The counselor who led him to Christ and finally brought him
to his senses convinced him that he was deceived. The same
counselor then fell in love with one of his counselees, divorced
his wife, and married his lover—all the time claiming that he
was doing the right thing.
Sin is terribly deceptive, and in the times of our deception,
anxiety actually becomes our friend. It refuses to lift until sin is
acknowledged and destroyed.
In such a time we can even be thankful for anxiety.
In such a time we can pray, as did David, that God will
reveal anxiety's cause.
Anxiety can be the result of real guilt or imagined guilt.
The Holy Spirit's responsibility is to place His sensitive,
invisible finger on real sin (John 16:8). Satan's devilish practice
is to whisper insidious reminders of sin already confessed or
sin never committed. He even magnifies feelings of overwhelming worthlessness and then uses those feelings to create
disabling anxiety (Revelation 12:10).

How does one distinguish between the Spirit's conviction and Satan's accusations?

The Holy Spirit is always specific. When He reminds us of sin, it's real sin with a time and a place. His promptings are fully detailed and accurate.

Satan generalizes. He likes to continually tell us we are sinners. He makes us feel sinful even after specific sin has been confessed.

David realized this and asked God to search his heart and then specify whatever deed could have caused his king to hate him so.

Anxiety can also signal the approach of a wrong decision.

During the Apostle Paul's second missionary journey, he was uniquely restrained from continuing his ministry in Asia.

> And they passed through the Phrygian and Galatian region, having been forbidden by the Holy Spirit to speak the word in Asia; and when they had come to Mysia, they were trying to go into Bithynia, and the Spirit of Jesus did not permit them; and passing by Mysia, they came down to Troas. And a vision appeared to Paul in the night; a certain man of Macedonia was standing and appealing to him, saying, "Come over to Macedonia and help us" (Acts 16:6-9).

Preaching in Asia had been Paul's calling to this point in time. The regions of Galatia and Phrygia needed Christ as did the area surrounding Ephesus. He was forbidden, not by the existent political powers, or by a dictum from his church, or even by a decison made with his companions. The restraint was internal. The Spirit of God overwhelmed him with a spirit of anxiety. He was restrained until a Macedonian call released him to move toward Europe.

Martha and I were invited to minister in central Honduras many years ago. The missionaries were excited about our coming, our church was enthusiastic and supportive, but we had no rest in our spirits.

Both of us were equally anxious. We didn't know why.

We prepared our itinerary, purchased our tickets, and began to pack. Two days before our departure, anxiety prompted us to cancel our plans. Of all the extensive ministry trips we have taken together, this was the only one we felt mysteriously constrained to call off.

The missionaries were disappointed, our church was bewildered, and we were confused.

Two weeks later we received word from the team on the field that the plane on which we were scheduled to fly into the interior had crashed in the mountains. Those who survived the disaster were killed by natives.

Thank You, Father, thank You for an anxious spirit that is designed to prompt us to search our hearts or God's.

"Friendly" anxiety can also signal a fractured relationship.

> If therefore you are presenting your offering at the altar, and there *remember* that your brother has something against you . . . (Matthew 5:23).

That's anxiety.

Nothing distracts from worship more than fractured relationships. In our most holy moments as we approach God, the Holy Spirit has a unique way of reminding us that before we can enjoy God, we must be fully right with man.

I watched recently as three people slipped from their places of worship in a Sunday morning service. They walked forward to a spot near the pastor, whispered something in his ear, waited for a response, and then returned to their seats.

Later I asked the pastor what happened.

"We had a rough business meeting this week," he said. "They all came to ask my forgiveness for some offensive remarks."

> If therefore you are presenting your offering at the altar, and there remember that your brother has something against you, leave your offering there be-

fore the altar, and go your way; *first* be reconciled to your brother and *then* come and present your offering (Matthew 5:23-24).

"Evidently they were distracted in their worship by the memory of what they'd said. They were just doing what the Scriptures told them to do," he said.

That's friendly anxiety.

John sums up friendly anxiety with the words,

Beloved, if our heart does not condemn us, we have confidence before God (1 John 3:21).

●

A restless, anxious heart can be an enemy quickly stilled by the quiet confidence that God is in control, or it can be a friend attempting to gain our attention with a message we need to hear.

Thank-You Therapy addresses that perplexity and is ultimately going to unravel the problem that prompted it.

Thank-You Therapy responds to an anxiety before its cause is known and soothes it before its cure is discovered.

Thank-You Therapy sometimes even thanks God for anxiety and then rests in peace as God reveals its cause.

QUESTIONS TO REFLECT ON
1. Is there a restlessness in your life for which you can find no explanation?
2. Have you thanked God for it?
3. Have you asked Him to reveal its source?
4. Do you need to seek counsel from a friend to help give you understanding?
5. Are you willing to do this?